Landscapes of a Mind:

A Collection of Fiction, Nonfiction, and a Novella

Sharon Penn

BALBOA
PRESS

A DIVISION OF HAY HOUSE

Balboa Press books may be ordered through booksellers or by contacting:

Balboa Press
A Division of Hay House
1663 Liberty Drive
Bloomington, IN 47403
www.balboapress.com
1 (877) 407-4847

Because of the dynamic nature of the Internet, any web addresses or links contained in this book may have changed since publication and may no longer be valid. The views expressed in this work are solely those of the author and do not necessarily reflect the views of the publisher, and the publisher hereby disclaims any responsibility for them.

The author of this book does not dispense medical advice or prescribe the use of any technique as a form of treatment for physical, emotional, or medical problems without the advice of a physician, either directly or indirectly. The intent of the author is only to offer information of a general nature to help you in your quest for emotional and spiritual well-being. In the event you use any of the information in this book for yourself, which is your constitutional right, the author and the publisher assume no responsibility for your actions.

Any people depicted in stock imagery provided by Thinkstock are models, and such images are being used for illustrative purposes only. Certain stock imagery © Thinkstock.

Print information available on the last page.

ISBN: 978-1-5043-5902-3 (sc)
ISBN: 978-1-5043-5903-0 (e)

Balboa Press rev. date: 06/29/2016

This book is dedicated to
My children and grandchildren.
I hope they enjoy the stories.

Please watch for my second
book, coming out soon,

**CHANGE 1 BEHAVIOR:
IMPROVE YOUR LIFE.**

It's a self-help book with proven ways of changing
or tweaking a behavior, so you can have a better
life.

It's easy to do because you focus on only one
behavior change until you succeed with that one
before you start on changing another.

Contents

BLANK CANVAS

Lisa's hands shook and her body trembled as she sat across from the school counselor. She wanted to tell Mrs. Swenson what had happened to her during the past two years; but she could not open her mouth, and her lips felt so cold, so numb. If she could get her lips to move, how would she be able to talk with her throat so tight and her mouth so dry?

She had wanted to tell the counselor about it ever since she saw how easily the other girls could talk to her. But Leo had told her what would happen if she said anything to anybody. He was so stern when he said it. He had been telling her the same thing for the past two years, ever since he started coming to her room at night, long after everyone else was sound asleep.

Lisa was so afraid—afraid of what Mama Sarah would do when she found out what was going on in her own home, with her own son. Lisa loved Mama Sarah and always wanted to please her, but mostly, she didn't want to hurt her.

When Lisa went to live in the Vincent home as a foster child she promised Miss Poe at social services that she wouldn't cause any problems that would get her moved to another foster home. She promised to always do what she was told, and isn't that what she had done? Miss Poe had told her that she didn't have any place else to live except with a foster family, because her mother was gone and there were no other relatives.

During the past two years, Miss Poe would visit her and ask her how she was doing. Before Lisa could get up the nerve to talk to the social worker, Miss Poe would ask the foster mother how Lisa was behaving in her home. Mama Sarah always reported that she had never had a girl who was so quiet, so good and who did what she was told to do. That seemed to satisfy the social worker, so she would leave, telling Mama Sarah to call her if there were problems. Lisa never said anything to anyone about her night visitor.

The school counselor was leaning forward, waiting for Lisa to tell her why she was here. Mrs. Swenson wasn't pressuring her; however, Lisa knew she had to begin talking before she lost her nerve again like she had done many times over the past two years. But, now was different—now Leo was gone. He said he was finished with her, and was going far away, probably to a tropical island so he could never be found. He knew that once Lisa told what had happened in the foster home, the police would be looking for him.

Lisa began speaking, "I was ten years old when I went to live with Mama Sarah. Miss Poe took me there. It was late at night; I had to wait a long time 'til she found me a place to stay. That day, my mother had stopped the car at an apartment building, and told me to go in there and ask the security guard to help me.

"My mother told me she had to go away for awhile and would return later to get me. She told me to ask the security guard to call social services. I did it because I knew my mother couldn't face the welfare people. They used to come to our place when someone would report us for not having food, or when we would be sleeping in the car when we didn't have any place else to stay. She would tell them she didn't need or want their help. They would make us stay at the shelter for the homeless when we didn't have a room, but Mommy didn't like it there. She said she would take care of us without their help.

"There were lots of times we were hungry, and even when we would be digging for food in the dumpsters outside restaurants, she would say she had her pride and would not ask for help."

Mrs. Swenson had heard Lisa's story from Miss Poe. She knew the child had gone into foster care looking frail—pale from her meager diet and from the trauma of her mother's abandonment that day. The social worker had described Lisa's appearance that day two years ago: the whiteness of her skin had an alabaster glow and her blonde hair was fine-textured, long and straight.

Although Lisa was withdrawn that night, Sarah Vincent, the foster mother, was warm and loving, experienced at helping the child feel right at home. She showed her the room that would be hers and offered her the fresh-baked brownies she had just taken from the oven, especially made for Lisa's "homecoming."

Lisa continued talking to the counselor, "I love Mama Sarah and I don't ever want to leave her; well, not until my mother comes back to get me. Anyway, now that Leo's gone, I can stay there, can't I?" While she searched Mrs. Swenson's face, the teacher reached across the desk to hold Lisa's trembling hand in her own.

"We'll see. Now tell me more about living with Mrs. Vincent."

"Well, about a week, maybe two weeks after I got there, Leo—that's Mama Sarah's son, he's 23, he came to visit. Mama Sarah said he wouldn't stay long so we wouldn't have to tell Miss Poe about it. One night—it was real late and I was already asleep—Leo came to my room. I watched him close the door through the slits of my eyes so he would think I was still asleep. He took the crazy quilt that lay at the foot of my bed and stuffed it at the bottom of the door. It was dark so he turned on the lamp by my bed, and moved the dresser in front of the door.

"He saw I was watching him and he whispered real quiet-like that he wouldn't hurt me. He said I would have to be very, very quiet so I could keep living with his mama."

Lisa's voice was shaking as she spoke, "I was so scared that night and didn't talk to him—that night and all the other nights after that. He talked while he was there, speaking softly, telling me what he wanted to do when he became famous. He never said anything about me not talking, and he never asked me questions, so I didn't have to answer him. He did ask me to call him 'Leonardo' when he was in my room, but I never did."

As Lisa talked, the counselor came from around the desk and sat down beside her, patting her often as Lisa told her about the past two years.

Mrs. Swenson's touch gave Lisa the courage to continue her story, "Leo would tell me that he always wanted to be an artist and show the world what talent he had. He would talk about the blank canvas being a challenge to him. Many times he would bring his sketches to my room and spend hours showing me his work. He would tell me about the famous artists whose work he admired. He would talk about the many years it took for them to become well-known, sometimes not until long after their deaths. He said he was too impatient to wait that long to become famous; he wanted the world to know his work now.

"After a while, I wasn't as afraid of Leo as I had been those first nights alone with him in my room. I never wanted him to be there, but I never told him to leave; I was afraid I'd have to move away from Mama Sarah."

Lisa was talking faster and faster. Finally, she stopped and Mrs. Swenson told her she wanted to call a friend of theirs, and told Lisa to stay where she was.

Soon, Miss Poe from social services and another woman, Detective Dunn from the police department came to the school. They spent a long time with the counselor in the school principal's office. When they came out, Detective Dunn and Miss Poe asked Lisa to go to the school clinic with them. Once they were there, the police detective asked Lisa to tell them exactly what Leo had done to her during those nights in the foster home.

Lisa thought that she could not tell all that had happened to her again so soon after telling Mrs. Swenson about it. She decided to show them; she started to cry softly as she unbuttoned her blouse, realizing she was now on display for the entire world to see. This was just what Leo expected would happen, just what he *wanted* to happen. Now he would be known in a way no other artist was known—not da Vinci, not Van Gogh, not Gauguin.

As Lisa removed her blouse, she held it in front of her small budding breasts, and turned for Detective Dunn and Miss Poe to see Leo's work. Her exposed torso was covered in brilliant colored tattoos: dazzling flowers, bright birds and animals, effulgent rainbows, pastoral mountains, gleaming ocean waves—a panoramic landscape.

The tattoos covered her torso. The placement of the pictures was well planned; no one had ever noticed the colorful drawings through Lisa's clothing. She was careful to dress conservatively, and due to her modesty, Mama Sarah had respected her privacy, always knocking on her bedroom door and waiting for permission before entering.

After Lisa was allowed to redress, Detective Dunn asked her about Leo's treatment of her when he was in her room. She said, "He let me cover myself as he worked. I only had to uncover the part of my body he was working on, or the part he wanted to look at. He would admire his work as he talked about how famous he would be once his own 'Mona Lisa' showed the world his masterpiece.

"When he came to my room, he brought me special treats--foods that I never had before, or small trinkets or a necklace, or another time, a ring he said he found. As he worked on the pictures, he told me stories about his dreams of traveling the world. It kinda relaxed me as he talked."

Detective Dunn asked many questions, having Lisa tell about her feelings during the time these experiences were occurring, getting her to reveal why she didn't feel she could tell anyone about what was happening. Then, as Lisa dressed and the social worker left the room, the detective told her that Miss Poe was making arrangements for Lisa to go to another foster home where she would be safe.

Lisa began sobbing. "But, I kept quiet all this time so I could stay with Mama Sarah." The detective explained to Lisa why Mama Sarah's home wasn't safe with Leo still at large.

Miss Poe came in to tell her that they would be leaving now to go to another foster home. Lisa continued sobbing as she looked up at Miss Poe, "See, I did what you said. I didn't cause any problems to have to get moved, and it's happening anyway."

Miss Poe looked at Lisa with tears in her eyes and told her, "I won't ask you to make any more promises, but I'll make one to you. I'll be there for you as long as I'm allowed to, and I promise to listen to you from now on."

Lisa continued crying quietly as her personal items were brought to her from her locker. She said goodbye to Mrs. Swenson who stood at the front door. Then, Lisa, Miss Poe, and Detective Dunn left the building. As they walked down the front steps and away from the school, the counselor heard Lisa ask Miss Poe, "May I go say goodbye to Mama Sarah and can I visit her sometimes?"

They were too far away for Mrs. Swenson to hear Miss Poe's reply.

End

Fiction

THE RIGHT STUFF

God knows, Snooky tried to get it right. And he'd be the first to tell you that—if he were still around. He always told me that families were the backbone of America. He sincerely believed that—bragged he'd been married five times and had kids in that many states.

He sounded so sincere when he talked about the importance of the family. I guess that's why I hitched up with him—that and my boy needed a man around.

Snooky never talked about the other wives; I can't remember that he ever called them by name. Once he saw a shaggy dog on the street and mentioned that "the wife" had a dog like that.

By that time, I had stopped asking about the past. At first, I had some questions, being the curious person that I am. Snooky would reply, "That part's over." He looked so free of it—like it never happened—so I quit asking. That and the fact that after a while I had begun to wonder about his sincerity.

Like when he talked about it was a man's place to earn the living so the wife could stay home and keep house. Well, after a couple of years, I was still working *and* keeping house; and he was still looking for the right job.

He took off last month. Funny, my boy hasn't asked any questions; but I guess I'll be wondering for a long time if Snooky will ever get it right someday, somewhere.

End

Fiction

THE CEDAR CHEST

As I sit looking at the cedar chest, I think of many of the memories it opens up. I am thinking how this chest holds some symbols of my past, present, and future in it. It has been with me for many years, and now it is time to pass it on.

First, my mother had the chest and she passed it to me when I finally got married back when I was 35 years old. At the time, she had a glint of humor in her eyes as she told me she had wondered if she was going to have the opportunity to give the chest to me, since she thought I might remain the proverbial old-maid school teacher.

"How time flies!" my mother would say to me when she was nearing 80. And, now as I approach that age, I agree with her, sometimes wishing I could recapture many of those happy times that flew by so fast.

I also wish I could change some of the sad times, or, at least, not remember them so vividly. As I sit here waiting for the person I will pass the chest on to, I remember the years that followed my marriage to Tom. I'm so glad I couldn't know the heartaches that would be in our future. And, I would never have expected all the joy that came out of the heartaches.

I open the chest to see the treasures that I have stored there. On top is the wrapped gift that I will give Millie, my beautiful granddaughter, when she comes by with her new husband to see me today as they arrive back from their honeymoon.

Under the gift are the baby clothes used by two generations, which I will pass on to her for the future so a third generation can wear the outfits. I slowly unwrap the delicate tissue paper from around the pale pastel dresses and gowns. I rub my finger over the little pink and blue satin rosebuds that were so carefully and lovingly crafted by my mother and her mother for my baby so many, many years ago.

When our daughter—our only child—and her husband died in a car accident, Millie, who was three years old at the time, was visiting us. She came to live with Tom and me and our watching her grow into a young woman so like her own mother was bittersweet. Sometimes the joy of her beauty and love was such a reminder of our loss.

Now I am alone. Tom and Millie are gone—Tom to wait for me in heaven and Millie to begin her life as a wife and later as a mother. Will she treasure the chest that I have kept for her? I had first given it to her mother, and then had to bring it home to wait for Millie to receive it? And will she appreciate the value of the gift I have for her?

I must have dozed off as I've been doing a lot of lately. There's the doorbell, and Millie's voice ringing out as she opened the door, "Grandmama, we're home; are you awake?"

As she came into the room with Jim, her young husband, she was beaming with happiness and anticipation. She rushed to greet me with a hug, "Oh, Gran, the islands were so beautiful, the sea so blue. I wish the honeymoon could last forever."

"It will, my love, it will," Jim said as he wrapped his arms around both of us.

They sat down on the sofa in front of me and we had a cup of tea, while talking about their trip. Then, I reached for the wrapped gift from the cedar chest, "This is something I want you to have to symbolize your love for each other and my love for you. I hope you will always keep it as a reminder of that love."

As Jim and I looked on, Millie ripped the paper from around the large square box. As she lifted the lid, I watched her face and held my breath as she looked down at the silver-framed wedding pictures of the three generations: Tom and me, her mother and father, and her and Jim. She let her breath out slowly and said, "You and Granddad were great parents to me after my mom and dad died, and now you have given me the greatest gift—a part of yourself and memories I will keep close in my heart always. Thank you."

As she laid the box of pictures down beside the wrapped baby clothes, I knew she had the past, present, and future together in that cedar chest as I had all those years ago, and was now passing on to her.

End

Fiction

DOWN THE MOUNTAINSIDE

She looked at him as if he were a stranger to her, not the man she had lived with for the past seven years. This was *not* her husband, standing there with the smug look of satisfaction after making his "declaration of independence."

One thing Tommy had always been was predictable. After they had been together for only a few months, he never did anything that Joan could not have anticipated would happen. And now he was telling her that he…

Wait! Is that the best way to start this story, or should we begin when Joan met Tom at that party at the Lawson's house? Joan got there late. Before she got introduced to all the people in the room, she could tell most of them wished they had some place else they had to be, and so did she. Then, Tommy walked into the room from the kitchen with a filled ice bucket.

Did I say *walked*? He had a way of entering a room that seemed as though he was just coming off the ski slopes, and was stopping by for a short time before continuing on down the mountainside.

He did that the night Joan met him—just glided over to her with the ice bucket still in his hands. "You're Joan; Meg wanted me here tonight to meet you. I told her I'd come if she promised she wasn't lying about her description of you. She wasn't; you're as beautiful as she said."

He put the ice bucket on the bar and took her hand, "Come with me; let's go out back, I want to show you something. The Lawson's St. Bernard just had five puppies and I want you to help me pick out one."

Joan's life changed that night when Tom entered the room and love entered her heart. Three whirlwind months later they were married and the pace never let up until this moment, this moment when the world seemed to stop spinning, this moment when Tom declared his independence.

There was no sound in the room except the street noises they heard through the open window and some far-off sounds of children playing in the park a block away.

This man standing here was telling her that he no longer wanted to work at the job he had claimed he thoroughly enjoyed. And he was saying that he did not want to live any longer in the house they had built together, selecting every piece of furniture together, and proudly showing off Molly, the St. Bernard they had gotten from the Lawsons.

Tommy said he was leaving and he told her that she could come with him if she wanted. He told her he did not know where he was going, but he had stayed too long in this one place; longer than he had ever stayed in any one place. He said he had only stayed this long because of her, but now he needed a change of scenery. He was walking out of the room as he spoke these last words. He said them boldly, in a loud voice.

Joan did not hesitate as she followed him; she hadn't expected him to invite her to go with him after he said he was leaving *everything* behind. She was thinking that she'd better get Molly and grab the snow skis to be ready for that ride on down the mountainside to the valley below.

End

EASTER BASKETS
EVERYWHERE

When Lisa's children were small, she loved this time of year when she would gather them around the kitchen table with newspaper spread out all over to catch the drips. Bowls of the dyes of different shades of blues and reds, yellows and greens were scattered out over the newspaper. The eggs had been cooked ahead of time and were cool to the touch. They rested in wire baskets amid the bowls of dye, ready for the small hands to lift them out carefully.

The children would whisper as they lifted the eggs out, one at a time, as though the sounds of their voices could possibly crack the delicate eggs if they spoke too loudly. Maybe it was the awe they felt as they created something so delightful and beautiful. They would use slotted spoons to dip them so slowly in the colors, making different shades by the length of time they kept each egg in the dyes.

The children's eyes would sparkle as they saw the egg change from the stark white to the color they had chosen. The giggles and laughter would start when they saw the magic that the white wax pencil created where they had drawn a design on the white egg before dipping it in the color.

As Lisa remembered those times, she realized how long it had been since she had children to share these precious moments with. Where had the time gone? Now, she had grandchildren and they would be visiting her at Easter for the first time. From pictures the parents sent her of the past Easters, she knew that the children got huge Easter baskets with lots of candy eggs, big chocolate Easter bunnies, fluffy stuffed animals and brightly colored *peeps*, all covered in bright, crinkly cellophane paper.

Maybe this year could be different. Maybe the parents would enjoy a return to the past, when things were simpler. She could set up the kitchen table spread with newspaper and have the many bowls of colorful dyes ready for them so the children could share a happy time with their parents and the mom and dad could share happy memories of their long-ago Easters. She smiled as she remembered the giggles and laughter from the past, and looked forward with anticipation to the happy times with them all together.

END

Fiction
GIVE THANKS

Helen rose from her chair at the kitchen table and walked across the room to the telephone. She picked up the receiver and listened for a dial tone. Sure enough, it was working; she wasn't sure because she hadn't heard it ring for many days. She was waiting to hear from her daughter, or her son, or maybe even her best friend, Margie, about plans for Thanksgiving.

She thought about the many holiday meals she had prepared for lots of people. Thanksgiving Day for her was a special day. At the dinner table, after Jim gave thanks to God for the food, she would ask their guests to tell what they were thankful for. She was pleased when everyone told of their many blessings. Then she would tell the story of her sad and lonely life until she met Jim, her greatest blessing. After they married and had their three children, she never had another lonely day.

Then Jim died. Her life after his death in January began to seem to her like her earlier years—quiet, lonely, little to do, and certainly, very sad. She just couldn't help but think that she should have died with Jim. What did she have to live for now that he was gone? Her children had their own lives; she was no longer useful to anyone.

Surely she would hear from someone inviting her to their Thanksgiving Day dinner. Tina, her oldest daughter, lived in Maine—that was a long way from sunny Florida, where she and Jim had raised their children. Maine is where Tina's job took her; she came home twice a year—at Christmas and during the summer—and she called often.

Kate, her middle child, was married to Joe; they had two teenagers who needed lots of attention. And Kate had that demanding job that kept her so busy she only ran over to see Helen on Saturdays to offer transportation if her mother didn't want to take the bus to go shopping.

Jimmy was her baby and her joy; he was so much like Jim that it hurt her heart to look at him. Last year, when he got married, Helen had to adjust to thinking of him as a grown man.

His wife, Julie was a sweetie who was close to her own family and wanted to spend holidays with them in North Carolina, where they all lived. Helen understood, but it didn't make the loneliness any less painful.

She would have to call Margie, her long-time friend, to see what her plans were. Margie had been alone for three years now. She had decided to remain in Florida after her husband died, although her sisters in Georgia begged her to move close to them. But, Margie was independent and never had a boring day. She had been urging Helen to join her in some of the many activities that kept her busy.

Today, when Helen called, she got her on the first ring, not having to leave a message. Margie was breathless from having just run in the front door from her latest project: she had joined a seniors' group who served meals to the homeless. She began telling Helen about the plans for feeding Thanksgiving dinner to

1000 homeless men, women, and children at the center downtown.

Helen knew immediately that this was how she would spend Thanksgiving Day—just as she had done for many years—feeding people and sharing their lives with each other. She would have a purpose again, and maybe she could be useful to others.

She couldn't wait to tell the children. After arranging a time to meet Margie at the Senior Center, she said goodbye. She picked up the phone again to hear the dial tone and to call Tina, Kate and Jimmy. What a great Thanksgiving Day they would all have!

End

Fiction

PANDAMONIUM
In the
CONDOMINIUM

We turned onto the street near our condo and saw what looked like hundreds of flashing blue and red lights in front of our building. I said to Mac, my husband who was driving the car, "Not again. I swear, if those guys don't stop their fights, they're *gonna* kill each other. The cop cars are everywhere and there's an ambulance. I wonder which one got hurt this time?"

Mac, shaking his head, said, "Possibly both of them. It's like they're training for a boxing match, and getting faster and better every time they get into the ring. I wonder what set them off this time?"

As Mac parked the car down the street from their door because the road was blocked with all the service cars, I said, "Maybe this time the two of them will go to jail for disturbing the peace. How can a place with only 20 units have such bad luck as to get two hot-tempered people in the same building—and both of them in their 70s. I don't believe they ever agree on anything."

As they walked up to their front door and Mac put the key into the lock, he said, "Some of the long-time residents say they used to be the best of friends and their wives were super close—like sisters. Now, they can't be in the same room together without a battle—either angry words or snide remarks. Neighbors say they've been at this for *years*. And the wives can't even speak to each other without the husbands' wrath."

"Well, they do talk to each other at the women functions, but I can tell they're not as comfortable with each other as I hear they use to be," I said as I looked out the window expecting to see those silly old men being forced into the back of the police car. Nope, nothing happening, except the police cars turning off their flashing lights and pulling out of the condo complex—without anybody sitting in the backseat. "Unbelievable!" I yelled out.

Mac, guessing correctly what I was yelling about, called from the bedroom where he was changing clothes, "What did you expect? We go through this fracas every few months and nothing happens; why do you expect that to change?"

I was silent; I had no answer for him. I never thought this would be the *adult activities* the flyer talked about when we first started thinking about moving into a condominium. We thought moving here would give us the freedom to travel—*just lock the door without a worry and go on your trip; everything will be taken care of.*

And then there were the friendships we expected we'd have with the neighbors as we played together—tennis and bocce ball on our own courts, swimming in our own Olympic size pool, games and potlucks in our private clubhouse.

I began thinking about last year: just when I thought we'd settled down and would never move again, we got this flyer from the realtor we liked and trusted—Lynn Box. As soon as I looked at it I knew I should have tossed it in the trash; it was a luxurious three-bedrooms, three-bath-condominium in Sunset View Condominiums. And the scenery was beautiful; it was located overlooking a large lake with sunsets to die for, and the breezes off the lake made you want to stay there on the screened porch from now on. A retiree's dream, right?

As we walked through the spacious, beautifully staged condo with Lynn, sunlight was streaming through the windows overlooking the sparkling lake, and I was already mentally placing our furniture. We sat on the porch talking with Lynn, who told us that the owners were highly motivated. She knew we could afford it from our previous real estate transactions with her, and she said she already knew someone who would buy our present home "in a heartbeat."

So, there we were on moving day. Many of our family and friends helped us pack up; the downside was that we had to take a razzing from those who had heard us say after the last move: "We. will. never. move. again."

When the moving truck got to the condo, the new neighbors showed up with food and drinks and in their work clothes—ready to help us get settled in and to party afterwards. As tired as I was that day, I thought about how everyone seemed to get along so well.

Well, I guess they had on their *company manners*; just a few days later the gossip began. It seemed some people couldn't wait to tell the new residents about the oddballs—gay men in one unit and possibly lesbians in another. The gay men liked to dress up in negligees and take pictures of each other. I didn't ask how the gossipers knew this; they appeared disappointed I didn't ask. The women who lived together denied being lesbians, so we called them "the girls" when we talked about them.

And then, there was Bonnie in Unit 15: she left the complex every Thursday to get her hair styled, but was gone for hours. There were different opinions about what she was doing all that time she was gone. Some of those people had vivid imaginations, and the stories they told could curl your hair—like Bonnie's new *do*.

Peggy, our next-door neighbor, told me matter-of-factly that Bonnie, a widow, had a standing appointment at a large adult condominium, a golf-cart community called Village Square, where the residents would engage in swinging parties; you remember, those gatherings of singles and married couples called *Swingers* that started in the '70s and are obviously still active today. Peggy seemed to know a lot about it and was eager to tell me the details as we sat drinking tea on her screened porch.

Peggy told me that Bonnie confided in her with details; told her that a married couple from our condo complex goes there, too, but she wouldn't tell her who it is. She said Bonnie told her, "There's a bar in that community that *features a drink called 'Sex On The Square' in honor of a woman who was arrested when she was caught having sex in public with a younger guy there. The drink is a fruity one, complete with whipped cream and a cherry on top.*

A journalist went undercover in that community *where there are hundreds of people--10 women to every man.* What he found was shockingly titillating, especially for senior citizens. They have a thriving seniors' swingers' scene – sorry for that mental image – and a black market for Viagra. I suppose you would need such in order to have an active swingers' scene in a retirement neighborhood.

Peggy said, "I read all this in the newspaper and online: There's supposedly a large group of those residents who have STDs, you know, sexually transmitted diseases." She lowered her voice when she said this, as though the rest of what she was telling me was just her talking about the weather.

I left with Peggy telling me to not repeat a word of this. I didn't promise her a thing; I was planning to tell Mac everything I'd heard. First, I had to Google what she told me to see if it was true, but what words do I Google? *Swinging Senior Sex Symbols?* Or maybe, *Old Codgers Chomping at the Bit?* Or, *Retirees Spicing It Up?*

When Mac got up from a nap, I told him everything Peggy told me and what I found out from my research online. He sat there, not interrupting, until I finished.

When he could speak, he asked, "Are you sure I'm awake, or am I having a weird dream? Is this really happening in this quiet rural county we moved to—to live out our years in 'God's Waiting Room'?"

We were curious—just curious; not interested. So, one night, we had dinner at a restaurant in the square, and a waitress told us about *key* parties for married couples at an Italian restaurant on Senior's Landing. She said, "Golf-cart, name-labeled keys get put in a fishbowl in the middle of the table, while women wait in the parking lot for their mystery dates. Also, a prostitution ring was recently broken up, and orgies are said to be a regular occurrence. This place is called 'Disney World for Old People'."

We were warned about women prowling around bars indiscriminately offering oral sex. The waitress said, "Sticking a loofah on your golf-cart antenna signifies you're into swinging. So does wearing a crimson button. According to multiple people, wearing gold shoes or letting your shirt tag stick out in the back signals you're on the prowl."

Our waitress was talkative; she had heard a story about a scorned woman painting large red letters on a man's garage door: "YOU FUCKING PRICK YOU GAVE ME HERPES!"

I had learned lots more in the year we had lived in the condo; YES, I had joined the gossip groups. I only had to hint at knowing a little bit about the mysterious swingers in our complex. All the women would talk when the men weren't around. Well, not *all*. I'd only bring it up when Rita wasn't around because I had found out early on that she and her husband, Phil were the married swingers.

They had moved to their condo here about four years ago, coming from that infamous condo community north of town. A few months ago Rita and I had become close when we went shopping together a few times.

Once, during lunch, I told her what Mac and I learned when we ate at Village Square, an ironic name, if you think about it. That's when she whispered to me that she and Phil go there, and how they got started in the activities. Phil found out about it and asked Rita to join him. She didn't agree at first, but after finding out that they'll take all the single women who apply, she figured she'd better join to keep an eye on Phil.

She said, "Many of the women told me they joined for the same reason, and then found out they liked it; that it had strict rules with no hanky-panky outside their circle. I never learned to like it; guess I'm too much a *Southern Baptist* to be comfortable with it."

She asked me not to talk about it with the other residents, so I don't; but some have guessed it's them. When the others discuss it, I'm quiet. The gossipers don't seem to notice that's one of the few times I'm quiet.

A couple of months after the cop cars and ambulance were at the condo when the men were fighting, we heard the sirens again. Mac asked, "Are they at it again?"

I was already at the window and saw the red lights flashing. "No, they've stopped down the street; I think the EMTs went into Rita and Phil's door. What could have happened?"

I stayed at the window, reporting any activity to Mac as it happened. "You should see all those nosy neighbors standing around out there!"

Mac laughed with a sarcastic tone; I knew that laugh. He was making fun of curious me, but I didn't care; I was worried about Rita. Finally, the responders came out with a body on the gurney. I told Mac, "It looks like Rita. I think she's alive, 'cause her head's not covered with the sheet."

As the ambulance pulled out with the siren on, Phil's car sped out of his garage, following right behind them. I grabbed my sweater and purse, "I'm going to the hospital. Rita and I have become friends and I'm going there for her. Do you want to go sit with Phil?"

The onlookers were still standing around outside, probably wondering what happened, when we left for the hospital. We went in through the ER automatic double doors where we found Phil sitting bent over with his head in his hands. I spoke quietly to him, "We came to sit with you and get you anything you need; just tell us."

He looked up at me then looked at Mac. "I can't think. Rita told me she was unhappy, but I didn't think it was this bad. I should have listened to her. What am I gonna do? I can't live without her; don't want to live without her."

We sat there, not asking any questions. Phil was quietly sobbing; I got up and got him some tissues from nearby. He thanked me and continued to cry softly. Mac got us coffee, and Phil held his cup but didn't drink from it; said he had too big of a lump in his throat.

Finally, after a long wait, the doctor came in and told Phil, "Your wife is stable for now; it was touch-and-go for a while. She was serious about this, but I think she's going to make it. I've got her sedated, so you can wait here until we get her settled in a room, and then you can go there. Someone will tell you when she's ready for you. Do you need to be examined or have meds?"

Phil shook his head so the doctor left. We sat a while then Phil looked at me and said, "Rita said she told you about our activities at Village Square. I guess she told you how distasteful it was to her. Well, this sure got my attention, so that's over for us. I sure hope she'll give me another chance so I can make it up to her. What do you think, Sue, do you think she will?

I just shrugged my shoulders as we got up to leave. I said to him, "Tell Rita I'll see her tomorrow morning. Call me if she needs anything." We walked out the double doors and went back home to our condo.

End

Fiction

THE PERFECT CHILD

If I could do it over again—knowing what I know now—how would I go about creating the perfect child?

I remember many years ago, long before I became a mother, I knew exactly what I would *not* do if I had children. Remember those days when you would talk about your friends who had children with those like yourself who had not yet begun the awesome journey of being a parent?

It was easy to say then, "When I have a child, I will never let him pull all those pots and pans out on the kitchen floor," or "I will *never* pick her up when she cries, only when she's being good," or "We will give him a certain allowance and if he spends it all, that's it!"

When the children came along our tune changed. Now we've joined the other parents who laugh at our childless friends who said things like: "My child will never act that way in public," or "She will always do her homework before watching TV," or "He will eat everything on his plate before having dessert."

Well I'm here to tell you that my children and my friends' children did all those things we said they would or would not do. But, of course, if you're a parent, you know that already.

When my children were young, I'd look at their beautiful angel faces—this was usually when they were sleeping—and I would get teary-eyed just thinking about those sad days when they would grow up and leave home to be on their own. I would think, *I don't believe I can stand it without them.*

And then came a change; they became *teenagers*. Oh, horrors! Are the teen years made for parents like I was—to help us stand the sorrow of the empty nest, to accept that there will be a good life after the children leave home? During those adolescent years, parents begin to pray for relief and begin to wish they had the nerve to run away!

Or, at the least, they started to count the days until this child, once again, believes that we—their mother and father—are not totally stupid; that we are able to function without their being there to direct us by saying, "Oh, Mother, REALLY?" Or "Please, Dad, don't tell that joke *again* to my friends."

Mark Twain's quote about the teen years would give us hope when we'd remember, in our despair, that he said, *"When I was a boy of 14, my father was so ignorant I could hardly stand him around. But when I got to be 21, I was astonished at how much the old man had learned in seven years."*

Well, I digress. The children do grow up, they do mature, and they do turn out okay. And they do make some good decisions that we like to take credit for. Also, they think we got smart again in our older years. That's a relief; Mark Twain was right!

So, now I'm back to the original question—if I could create the perfect child, how would I go about doing it?

Well, that's easy; it's already happened. And there he comes up the walk to my house—*my grandchild.*

End

Fiction

WOMAN'S WORK

"Why can't a man be more like a woman?" That ditty from years ago kept pounding in her head ever since she left the office late this afternoon and headed for the delicatessen.

She had to rush to get the food for dinner before the shop closed. And the ditty kept beating on with the passing cars, "Why can't a man be more like a woman?"

Janet turned her car into the parking lot of the deli just minutes before closing time. She jumped out, grabbing her purse, and rushed in, just in time to see Mr. Gibbs untie his apron and loosen it from around his ample belly.

He smiled at her as she walked through the door, "I knew you'd get here. I told Martha—that

Ms. Blaine won't let me lock the doors with her party food setting inside here."

After Janet paid him and set the trays on the car seat beside her, she eased back into traffic wondering, *why do I do this? Will I ever learn that I don't have to do it all?*

The ride home was relaxing—traffic flowed along at a steady pace. Janet always used this time to reflect on her workday or her plans for the evening or weekend.

Tonight, she and Jeff would be feeding and entertaining three couples they met in their therapy group. Their last session together was a month ago and they had decided, at that time, to get together later to talk about whether they thought the therapy was working for them.

Was it working? She and Jeff began therapy because they were always in a power struggle, fighting over the silliest things—like, who was to take out the trash, or whose turn to do the laundry. Life was simpler when she was growing up in a mom-stayed-home-while-dad-went-off-to-work kind of family.

Jeff's family life was different: He and his mom struggled to stay together, after his dad left—a two-against-the-world kind of family. His mom catered to him, doing everything for him as if to make up for his dad not being there for him.

Now, after a year of marriage, Janet and Jeff had been trying to find their own kind of family, and both had been struggling with the do-it-my-way theme. It had not been working, and so the reason for therapy.

As she stepped out of the shower, dried off, and reached for her deodorant, the ditty came back to her: Why can't a man be more like a woman?"

They learned the answer in therapy: there are no particular jobs for each partner, only what works for each couple. And that is always changing as circumstances change.

Jeff sometimes helped his single mom with chores because she had to work to support the two of them after his dad left. When he "forgot" or rushed the chore by doing it poorly, his mom didn't complain or discipline him. Janet always had her mom at home to take care of her and her dad. So, she thought now, that it was her place to handle all the housework including cooking and cleaning like her mom did and Jeff's place was to take care of finances and outside chores, like her dad did. Well, she was learning that ALL the chores were negotiable since they both worked jobs and each was good at or liked to do certain things.

Therapy had helped them sort out the best plan for them. It helped them to hear how other couples worked it out and to have a therapist give them guidelines for sharing the chores. She thought, 'I guess it's true—therapy is education.' And she also remembered the therapist saying, "If you do what you've always done, you'll get what you've always got."

Janet heard Jeff come in so she ran to greet him with a big hug, just like her mom always did with her dad. And Jeff had a big bouquet of spring flowers for her—also just like her dad did for her mom.

Janet thought how they would have lots to talk about tonight with the other couples—about the many changes they were making and the many things they didn't want to change because they worked so well for them.

End

THE BIG 'C'

Well, here I am again, sitting in the room with pastel walls. It's that time of year when I come to sit around with the other women. It could look like a woman's jewelry or Tupperware party except for two things. We are all dressed in matching pink pastel smocks. And, unlike at a party, you don't hear the chatter and laughter of the different-aged women. Each of us sits here, waiting our turn, seldom talking to the other women, turning pages in the magazines, and looking up every time someone walks into the room.

Yes, once again, I join other women for our annual trek to the Mammogram Center where everything has been planned to be soothing, from the pink and turquoise walls here in

Florida to the up-to-date magazines focusing on women's issues.

Only this year is different. This year I have just learned that a friend, fifteen years younger than I, has breast cancer. One day all is well, then the routine mammogram shows a mass, and lives are changed in an instance. Just that quickly, plans must be changed, schedules adjusted, and concerns for the future of a child must be faced.

As I go off to get the annual mammogram, my friend goes for a radiation treatment. She goes alone to prove that she can, which was her response when I offered to go with her.

I'm waiting for my name to be called. To distract myself, I flip through a magazine. On one of the back pages of a magazine filled with recipes and decorating tips is a full-page advertisement for a cancer treatment center—the first I've ever seen. Have they been there and I didn't notice? I consider writing the phone number down, but a superstitious feeling makes me leave the number in the book.

My name is called and I go into the x-ray room. In a pleasant but very professional manner, the technician gives me instructions for the four pictures that she will take. When she has finished she directs me back to a different waiting room where coffee and dainty cookies are set out as though we are at a social gathering.

I wait for the results of my mammogram, and try not to stare at the other women. How many of the women who come to the Mammogram Center each day will get the news that they have a suspicious mass? How many women discover it on their own, at home?

As I wonder, I overhear one of the technicians make a call, "Miz James, Dr. Logan wants you to come back for some more x-rays to be taken from different angles than the ones we took yesterday."

I was surprised when the technician did not have to answer any questions, and ended the conversation with scheduling an appointment. I think I would have a dozen questions, but maybe this woman had already asked the questions earlier. Or maybe she had no questions because she wasn't ready for the answers.

After a short wait my name is called. A different technician takes me to a darkened room with the x-rays already up on the screen. This is different; why are they doing this? They've never done this before, why now? Before I could panic and ask the questions, she begins to tell me that everything looks normal; there are no masses. I want to hug this stranger, but I merely smiled at her—a huge smile. She then directed me to the area to get dressed. Who will be the next one to get the bad news in this regular roulette routine?

I leave the building and notice what a beautiful day it is and how gloriously happy I am to be free of the big C—at least for another year.

End

Nonfiction

THE BLUES BUSTERS

DOWN IN THE DUMPS? NEED A LIFT OUT?
YOU MAY NEED THE BLUES BUSTERS.

Try these easy-to-do activities to decrease depression. Just pick a favorite—one a day and then get started.

Take a walk—or try another regular exercise, preferably with people you like to be with. The feeling of well-being produced by exercise is probably due to the release of endorphins, the body's natural painkiller. Regular exercise also raises your metabolism, which energizes you. Exercising with other people does two things: socializing discourages isolation, and it can help assure you will continue the program.

Schedule social events—go to a ball game, a funny movie, a concert, or participate in a sport. Discover what you enjoy doing and make time for it. Also, it's much more fun when you do it with people you like.

Work at having close, loving relationships—research has shown that of all the characteristics that happy people share, loving relationships seem to be *the most important*. Give special attention to the people you love. And, yes, you do have to work at it.

Create successes for yourself—get a new outfit, start a new project, or get a fresh start on a long-delayed chore. Sometimes, just the act of starting something new can give you a feeling of pleasure. *"Whatever you can do, or dream you can do, begin it. Boldness has genius, power, and magic in it."* Goethe

Help someone in need—a disadvantaged child, a homeless person, the elderly. Or cook a dish or a meal for a neighbor, friend, or co-worker. It's possible that altruism builds happiness in two ways: it enhances self-esteem and may relieve both physical and mental stress. Also, you'll enjoy the feeling of helping someone else feel good.

Treat yourself to pleasures—eat a favorite food, take a hot bath, read an uplifting book. Use this as a reward, a change of pace, or just when you need a lift. Remind yourself often that you are special and deserve the best.

Practice self-talk—it's important, and it also helps that when you do self-talk, to call yourself by name while looking in the mirror as you say an affirmation.

Affirmations are proven methods of self-improvement. They can "rewire" the brain. Make them positive statements and in the now. Put them on 3 x 5 index cards and place them near a mirror you will use to say them to yourself every day. Say your name as you say the affirmations to yourself.

Examples:

"I am unique, therefore I am awesome."

"I am happy and proud to be me."

"Creative energy surges through me and leads me to new ideas."

"Happiness is a choice. I base my happiness on my own accomplishments and the blessings I've been given."

"Today I abandon my old habits and take up new, more positive ones."

"I have achieved greatness."

"I love and accept myself for who I am."

"I am brimming with energy and overflowing with joy."

"I believe I can do everything."

"I forgive those who have harmed me in my past and peacefully detach from them."

Get out your coloring book—coloring is a low-stress activity that allows an individual to unlock their creative potential. More importantly, it helps relieve tension and pent-up anxiety because it unlocks memories of childhood and simpler times. Carl Jung, 1875-1961 [founder of analytical psychology] had his patients color in mandalas—a spiritual symbol in Indian religions—as a way of getting people to focus and allow the subconscious to let go.

Express Appreciation—give someone a compliment--a warm fuzzy. Choose a family member, a co-worker, or a friend, and tell them something that makes them special to you and others. Or write a letter to a person from your past who was unique in your life. Or write a thank-you note to someone you've heard of who has helped people in the community. You can do some of this online, if you have an e-mail address, or have social media.

Write in a "gratitude" journal on a regular basis; shoot for daily if possible. This helps you see all the positive things around you that you might have missed if you weren't looking for them. Write on your computer, or in a spiral notebook, or on 3 x 5 index cards. To keep it interesting, share in social media and others can share with you.

Set aside time everyday for prayer or meditation--researchers found that people who pray to a loving and protective God are less likely to experience anxiety-related disorders: worry, fear, self-consciousness, social anxiety and obsessive compulsive behavior, compared to people who pray but don't really expect to receive any comfort or protection from God.

A recent study found that participating in regular meditation or other spiritual practice actually thickens parts of the brain's cortex, and this could be the reason those activities tend to guard against depression — especially in those at risk for the disease.

Take one step at a time—out of the dumps and on to that great feeling. Choose one activity and when you do that one, notice immediately that you begin to feel better. If it seems like a lot to do, just try one a week until you feel better; then do one a day. At the end of the week, you will probably want to start over.

If your depression is mild, these actions are *guaranteed* to lift your mood. If the blues hang on for a few weeks, you may have more than a case of the blues; it could be a severe depression. You can still do the Blues Busters, but please see a mental health professional or your family doctor right away. Help is available.

Therapy is education. Sometimes, depressed people do things that make them more depressed because no one ever taught them a better way. *"If you do what you've always done, you'll get what you've always got."* J. Potter

A good therapist can teach you new skills for living a more productive and satisfying life.

DON'T DELAY; GET MOVING, AND ENJOY LIFE AGAIN

Nonfiction

BOOST YOUR SELF-ESTEEM

What is self-esteem and how do we get it? We usually know when we've got it, and when we don't. Knowing *how* to get it when we don't have it is more elusive.

What? You don't always know when you've got it? Well, just feeling good about yourself is one indicator.

When you can answer "Yes, often" to these questions, then you can be confident that your self-esteem is high:

- *Are you honest with your feelings when dealing with others?*
- *Are you making an attempt to resolve issues in your life?*
- *Do you volunteer to help others who are needier?*

- *Do you have good eye contact with others?*
- *Are you compassionate of other's plights in life?*

Your self-esteem may be low when you answer "Yes, often" to these:

- *Do you anger easily and is your anger often misdirected?*
- *Are you a smoker or over-eater, or do you abuse alcohol or drugs?*
- *Are you often ill with colds or other minor illnesses?*
- *Do you often find yourself telling a lie or a half-truth?*
- *Do you ever see yourself as a victim, or do you often feel victimized by other people's actions?*

Your answers to these ten questions may vary from day-to-day, according to Margaret Click, PhD, in her article, "Self-Esteem" (unpublished). She says, "It is easy to feel worthy and good about ourselves when things are going well. The trick is to have the seeds of the positive self-love, self-image, and self-awareness so deeply planted and well-fertilized within us that we feel worthy, compassionate, and loving toward ourselves even when, and *especially* when events are not going well."

The good news is that you can boost your self-esteem so you are prepared for those times when you have a setback. When the boosters become habits, then you are fortified and prepared for any event that happens in your life.

So, if you think your self-esteem needs boosting, try these tips for starters:

Do something every day that you do extremely well. No matter how insignificant it may seem, any accomplishment bolsters self-esteem. It may be something as simple as working a crossword puzzle, or cooking a dish you're famous for and sharing it with a neighbor or co-worker, or finding a new game to play with your family.

Learn something new every day. It may be as easy as learning a new word that you read in the morning paper or heard on the evening news. You may read something new that you want to share with your spouse, child, or co-worker. The more you know, the more interesting you are.

Do whatever it takes to make you feel good about yourself. It may be something easy like trying a new makeup or buying a new outfit. You can try an exercise workout with high-energy music, or take a walk with your i-pod or smart phone. Whatever helps, do it.

Cultivate people whose accomplishments you admire. Men and women who have succeeded at something—be it head of a company, a top producer in sales, or a great relationship with their spouse or children—have some secrets that they are usually happy to share. They are generally receptive to friendly overtures and welcome your interest and admiration of them.

Put out of your life anybody who puts you down. No matter who that person is, the relationship isn't worth it if it makes you miserable. Tell the person exactly what bothers you; if there's no change or the person refuses counseling with you, say "goodbye." Don't let anyone louse up the only life you have. If *you* are putting *yourself* down—stop it! Critical thoughts destroy self-esteem as effectively as positive thoughts build it.

Concentrate on the things you like about yourself. Find something that people comment on about you, and then play it up. Whatever your specialty is—be it hair, eyes, smile, creative ability, personality, or other—use it freely and often. And think about it anytime you are feeling down.

If you can change the things about yourself that bother you—do it now. If you need to lose weight, quit smoking, start exercising, get out of debt, move to another job—do it. And, do it now—right now, one day, one step at a time.

If what bothers you is something you can't do anything about—your height, race, origin, or some other unalterable state—stop brooding about it. Accept it and go ahead with your life. Seek out information about famous people who have the same trait, reminding yourself that it didn't keep them down, so it can help you, too.

Give thanks. And, most of all think often about things that you're grateful for. This helps you realize how special you are. Keeping a daily gratitude journal helps you focus on your blessings; you will be more mindful as you think about what will go into your journal. You can use a spiral notebook or a fancy bound book to write in, or use the computer to record your thoughts.

Self-esteem is based on your thoughts, feelings, and beliefs about yourself. When you believe you can do something, you have a better chance of success. When you tell yourself you can't do something, you increase your chance of failure. The next time you're up against a challenge, think positive thoughts for success.

"If you think you can or you think you can't, you're right." Henry Ford

FROM HOT-HEAD
TO COOL DUDE

A young mother in Tulsa, enraged after an argument with a neighbor, returned to her home and vented her anger by stabbing her three-month-old son to death. She told police detectives that she was angry after the argument and needed to take it out on someone.

In schools across the country, principals and security guards roam the halls and grounds on the lookout for fights and potential outbursts. Teachers frequently have to call for help when they see children lose control of their feelings when angered.

Mary J,* a 29-year-old single mother lives in Florida with her three children, Jenny, Sam, and Nell. She was recently reported to the state agency that investigates child abuse because she was frequently seen and heard hitting Jenny, age eight, and Sam, age six. She often left two-year-old Nellie alone in the apartment with the two older children when the sitter didn't arrive in time for her to get to her job as a sales person in a department store. *names changed

She had no family in the central Florida town where she had lived for the past year since she had left her abusive husband.

Mary was surprised that anyone would report her for abuse, saying she spanked her children to make them mind her; that she wasn't abusing them, but teaching them to be good kids. She did not want to acknowledge that her son had hit the two-year-old, and often got into fights with his older sister.

She considered herself to be a good mother, supporting her children and taking care of them without any help from their father or the welfare department. She left her husband when she realized he would not change—he would hit her and the children and then beg her to forgive him, over and over. Finally, she left.

She wonders how she had the strength to go, after living with the abuse for so long.

Violence in the home is common; what are the effects of domestic violence on children?

- More than 3 million children witness domestic violence in their homes every year.

- Children who live in homes where there is domestic violence also suffer abuse or neglect at high rates (30% to 60%).

- Children exposed to domestic violence at home are more likely to have health problems, including becoming sick more often, having frequent headaches or stomach aches, and being more tired and lethargic.

- Children are more likely to intervene when they witness severe violence against a parent – which can place a child at great risk for injury or even death.

Also, children are exposed to high levels of violence through television and movies. As child abuse and domestic violence reports increase, and children observe bloody battles all around themselves, both in the media and in their own homes and neighborhoods, will they assume that force is the only way to resolve conflicts? Can they be taught another way? Are parents whose childhoods were shaped through fear and force, able to learn a better way to teach their children that anger can be controlled and managed so that no one is harmed?

Before parents can teach their children about anger control, they have to learn for themselves the facts about the emotion that has caused so much grief and pain. Mary agreed to attend parenting and anger-management classes, and later said she never knew there was another way to discipline her children other than the way she was disciplined as a child. "I thought that I had to hit them to make them mind me; that's how my mom did it. I remember getting the belt on my back when I would sass her. I know I hit my kids many times when I was angry, and I called it 'doing it for their own good.' And I'd tell them that it hurt me more than it hurt them. Now, I'm learning how to control my anger, and I don't hit them anymore."

In Mary's classes, she learned some basic facts about anger: It's an integral part of a person; if denied or repressed, it will emerge in destructive ways, often unexpected. We must recognize its signals, know when we are feeling it, and try to locate its origins. To that, we have to stop ourselves immediately from acting on the feeling, and try to figure out where it's coming from. This takes a lot of practice, but we can learn to take time out to sort out the feeling and the way we plan to express it.

There are several ways we express our anger which we learn from watching others when they are angry: We adapt to these styles because we've been taught that this is how to express anger and possibly because our behavior has been reinforced in some way.

Sometimes we *hide* our anger when we don't want to directly confront the person or situation that is provoking the anger. However, it is expressed anyway in the form of sarcasm, unintentionally forgetting to do something for someone, holding back love, or avoiding the person or situation in the future. Hidden anger is hard to recognize because the *hiders* deny that they are angry, even when confronted. Hidden anger results in many physical and mental illnesses such as ulcers, migraine headaches, obesity, and depression.

Inflating is much easier to identify than *hidden*. *Inflators* usually begin their sentences with YOU; they blame *anybody* but themselves for their problems, they blame their spouse or children for the problem, they rant and rave at anyone who is nearby, and they can attack physically, usually anyone who is smaller and more vulnerable than themselves. People who are *inflating* may get their way, but only in the short run. Our opponents may give in to avoid our fury, but they will get back at us somehow, even in a disguised manner.

Handling our anger is a productive style because we clearly and appropriately express to the provoking person that we are angry at him or her. People who express their anger directly get their message across, feel closer to others, communicate better, and generally feel as though they have made contact in a personal manner. The more aware we become of how our anger is expressed, the more control we have over dealing with it.

Be aware of the dangers and limitations of *inner directed* anger which can cause depression. *Displaced* anger, which is directed at an inappropriate target, reminds us of a story of the man who went home and yelled at his family, or kicked the dog after his boss yelled at him at work.

You can begin immediately to practice anger management, and should do starting right now. Why wait? The next time you feel the emotion, you can "get physical"—take a long, fast walk, or go for a bike ride, or use an exercise machine, or scrub floors or walls, or tear up old magazines.

Some other ways are also effective: write about your anger, either in a journal or in letters you tear up. Talking with a friend or therapist will help you understand the specific cause of your anger, and crying releases the frustrations. (Don't spread it around on social media—it can create a problem if it gets to the wrong person.) Deep breathing and meditation help muscles to relax and resolve the physical component of your anger.

Modeling appropriate anger control is the best way for your children to learn how they can handle their own feelings. Karen T.* has an eight-year-old son, Tim, who stayed in trouble with the neighborhood children because of his temper; he just could not keep his cool when he was playing with them. She believed that he had inherited these strong feelings from his father, but she also blamed herself because of her behavior toward him. During the period following her divorce, Karen was under much stress because of financial problems and the uncertainty of her and her son's future, and she seemed to take it out on Tim. With professional help, she learned better ways to control her behavior, and new ways to help her son.

In addition to modeling the correct way to express emotions, Karen learned there are techniques and tools especially designed to help children learn the best way to act.

ChildsWork/ChildsPlay publishes a catalog with items which addresses the behavioral, social, and emotional needs of children, to be used by both parents and counselors. There are books, games, and workbooks which use activities to help children and teens learn nonaggressive alternatives to conflict. The free catalog can be ordered on line at their website ChildsWork.com, or call 1-800-962-1141.

Karen recently completed her counseling; on the last day with the therapist she reported that Tim said he wishes everybody knew how to tell others how they feel in a way that doesn't get them into trouble. Both Karen and Tim have found new ways to express themselves when they have stress. They now feel good about themselves and the way they relate to each other and other people in their lives.

And, remember Mary from our first success story after she was in her parenting and anger-management classes? Now she's helping to teach those classes, and brags about helping young parents learn new and better ways to discipline their children, and, most of all, to control their feelings before they get out-of-hand.   End

*Names are changed for privacy.

A VISIT TO THE HYPNOTIST

What varied reactions I got when I told several friends that I planned to visit a hypnotist for the first time!

"When you learn how to hypnotize, I want you to do me," said Anna. Marta asked, "That's spooky, will anyone else be in the room with you and him when you're under?" And Sue wanted to know, "Aren't you afraid you might not come out from under? What if he tells you to do something illegal?"

Well, I've been there and I'm back, and I can answer all of their questions.

As I drove to the address that Dr. M. gave me when I made the appointment, I was… excited, apprehensive, skeptical…yes, a little of all that. I was remembering the doctor's advertisement that caught my eye: "If You're Ready for a Change, Try HYPNOSIS!"

Could hypnosis really help me change my eating habits so that I could lose weight? And how about the motivation to exercise—can a hypnotist helps me *want* to exercise?

As I searched for the address Dr. M. had given me, I remembered he had told me that he shared the space with another business. I pulled up in front of the building with the address he had given me—What—a beauty salon?

Yes, Dr. M.'s office was in the back room of the salon. Going into a room full of women who were doing their beauty routine and gossiping about the latest happenings in their world took a lot of intestinal fortitude. But, I had come this far and nothing would stop me now!

One of the operators pointed to the back of the room when I asked for Dr. M., and I quickly headed there without glancing back to see the looks on the suddenly-quiet salon customers' faces.

As I turned the corner of the hall, I came face-to-face with a small, deeply-tanned man in white shirt and shorts, white socks and athletic shoes, looking like he had just come from playing in a tennis match. Except for the outfit, he looked surprisingly like Dr. Sigmund Freud, the psychoanalyst, complete with a salt-and-pepper beard and a stern and somber look on his face.

After introductions, I followed him into his small office, complete with diplomas and certificates on the white walls, and a bookcase full of books, tapes, and pictures. Two matching lounge chairs sat side-by-side with a rolling chair facing them. As the doctor directed me to one of the lounge chairs and he sat on the rolling chair, he asked me to fill out a one-page form.

I settled into the chair and began to complete the form while firing questions at him about his credentials and experience. He answered the questions in a subdued manner, and then his mood changed as he began a presentation about how the mind and body work together. He repeated several times, "What the mind perceives, the body believes."

The hour went by rapidly as he talked nonstop about the conscious and subconscious; how we learn and how we are conditioned. He would insert jokes or funny comments meant to relax me, I'm sure. About every 15 minutes, he would lift his arm up high and say, "Take a deep breath and let it out slowly, allowing it to flow down and throughout your body." His arm would flow down as he spoke. Then he would pick up his narrative and continue on, sharing his knowledge about the mind-body connection.

He said that we are all conditioned by our experiences and can recondition ourselves through hypnosis. However, before this can happen, we have to want to make the changes.

He discussed the myths that the public has about hypnosis. He said, "The fear people have about doing something while hypnotized that they would not normally do does not happen." He jokingly said, "If I had that kind of power, my wife would follow my commands. She is living proof that it is not going to happen."

As I laughed at one of his many jokes, I suggested that he could be a stand-up comedian. Turns out that he does have a comedy routine and will speak to groups for a minimal charge. Back in his hometown up North he was a minor celebrity with his act and has made a video which he sells. He reportedly did not nor does he now use hypnosis in his comedy act.

On the office wall, he has a picture of himself walking barefoot over hot coals. He explained, "I was able to do this by totally focusing my attention away from my bare feet and into my clinched fist. During the incident, I did not feel the hot coals nor did I have any burns from the experience." Again, he reminded me, "What the mind perceives, the body believes."

About halfway through the session, he rolled his chair over toward me and asked what I wanted to work on with hypnosis. He generally assists people with pain management, weight control, and smoking cessation. He said many people report to him how much he has helped them with their problems.

I told him I wanted to work on weight control and motivation to exercise. He shared his weight control program saying, "It is natural because you eat what you enjoy and enjoy what you eat.

It's based on a healthy mental attitude and eating properly."

"As you begin a meal, take a deep breath and as you slowly exhale, say to yourself, t*his is easy.* Continue to say this until you believe it, because *what the mind perceives, the body believes.* Remember: Relax, focus on the food, eat slowly and drink water, enjoy, and push the plate away when satisfied.

"If you do the program consistently, you will develop a habit of eating slowly while relaxed. Combine it with the following simple exercises and you will lose weight and volume at the same time.

"Exercise is helpful in maintaining a healthy body. But you don't lose weight by exercising. Walk a mile and you burn 100 calories. To lose one pound you have to burn 3500 calories. You will have to walk 35 miles without eating or drinking anything in order to lose one pound. By exercising, you lose volume, not weight. Fatty tissue is four times the volume of muscle."

One example of Dr. M.'s exercises is for the thighs: "In a sitting position, keep feet together, flat on the floor. Spread knees apart. Imagine you have a spring (like Suzanne Sommer's thigh buster) between your knees that is hard to compress. With that in mind, try squeezing the spring and release. Squeeze and release. You can do the exercises while watching television or talking on the phone.

"Maintaining a proper mental attitude is most important." Dr. M. said, "Every morning before getting out of bed, clench your fists as tight as possible and with enthusiasm say, 'I feel grrreat'—just like Tony the Tiger of Kellogg cereal fame. Your body will respond. Then get up and do a few minutes of flexing the muscles." Dr. M. said he does this every day and he feels grrreat!

After receiving all this information and his telling me several times to "take a deep breath and let it out slowly, down through the body," I was pretty well relaxed. He suggested I close my eyes and count to three: one…two…three…. He "tested" my relaxation by lifting my wrist slightly and letting it drop back down to the arm of the chair to see if I was "under." He had told me earlier that I would be aware of everything going on around me, and I did notice the voices of the salon customers and outside noises.

During this time he again went over his weight-control plan and exercise program. After some time, he told me that when I was ready, I should count to three and then open my eyes: one…two…three…. I was amazed that I did open my eyes on the exact count of *three*.

Nothing seemed different except I was relaxed, as though I had just finished a light nap. That evening, when I was ready to have dinner, I tried the doctor's method of relaxation and drinking water. The food did taste better and I ate less because I ate slowly and was aware of the taste of each bite. His suggestions had worked. Now, we'll see if they work over time.

It will take awareness at all times until the changes become habits. It will take remembering each day, each meal, each snack and by reconditioning my eating and exercise habits. Do I really want to make the changes? We'll know soon. Like Dr. M.'s joke: how many hypnotherapists does it take to change a light bulb? Only one—but the light bulb has to want to change. End

TALKS WITH MAMA

Have you ever noticed how birds appear to stand at attention, lined up around the edge of a pond, as if waiting for some sort of event to begin? They look around for awhile and then turn away, look down and wander off, or flying off in all directions as though they've lost interest in what brought them there.

I was so intent on watching the birds from my car and reflecting on their behavior that I was startled at the sound of a car horn behind, blasting at me for holding up traffic. I quickly turned right onto First Street, into a neighborhood that, until a month ago, was as foreign to me as the North Pole would be to the southern birds I had just been observing. The early autumn breeze was cool and gentle which made it pleasant to leave the office as I went out to visit a family I was assigned to in the social services department.

I had completed my degree in June, and got a job soon after in the state welfare department. After the training program, Mrs. Nelson, the supervisor, spent time reviewing each family's circumstances with me, answering questions, and encouraging me to shadow experienced workers to learn their social worker techniques. Now, after several months, the supervisor, who always had workers with crises lined up outside her office, told me I was on my own, but she'd be available, when needed.

The birds would soon be heading further south to avoid cold weather. Because I was alone in a different part of town than I had worked in over the summer, I was a bit anxious, and briefly wished that I too, like the birds, would be headed someplace else. But then, my apprehension was replaced by the anticipation of getting to know the Rayburns*, a family with young children. *Name changed for privacy.

There was no one on the street as I pulled up to the curb in front of the Rayburn's home. The shanties--rows of identical unpainted houses, all with small front porches, stood so close together they almost appeared to touch each other. Their proximity seemed to give them the fortitude to stand against time, although the poor construction and the unpainted siding were indicators of their limited lifespan.

As I locked my car and turned toward the house, I spotted three children peeking at me through the tattered-screened door. Their expressions remained somber while their eyes watched as I climbed the front steps and smiled at them, "Is your mama home? Tell her Ms. Mill's here from the welfare office."

Before the children could respond to me, Mrs. Rayburn called out from the front room, "Come on in; the door's open. Move out the way, younguns, so's the lady can git in."

The children scattered as I reached for the latch and pushed open the squeaky door. Mrs. Rayburn was standing at one of the two double beds in the room, folding quilts and smoothing the sheets. As I introduced myself, Mrs. Rayburn continued to busy herself with the beds, turning to acknowledge me by nodding her head but not making eye contact.

I turned to the children and said to them, "I know your names are Mary, Connie, and Jessie," pointing and smiling at each one as I said their names. They all giggled and tucked their heads down, putting their hands in front of their mouths in unison, as though they had rehearsed this gesture together.

The mother finished straightening the beds, told the children to stay where they were, and then led me through a door to another room which she called the parlor. "Come on in; I've about finished the wash and hung up the last few pieces." I could see into the kitchen where rows of wet laundry were hanging from cord strung back and forth from wall to wall, filling the kitchen. A wringer-type washing machine stood next to the sink with water still inside.

Because it was such a beautiful day, I was curious about the laundry hanging inside the house. As if she had heard the question, Mrs. Rayburn spoke, "When the wash hangs outside, the birds leave droppings and we have to rewash.

"Anyway, I don't like to go outside much. I stay inside with my children, the ones that's here now. Mary and Jessie will go off to school next year and then it's just me and Connie. She'll have to go to a special school 'cause she's slow, you know."

The mother talked at a steady pace, hardly taking time to catch her breath. I stood by, not wanting to interrupt her; glad I didn't have to draw out information from her as I'd had to do so many times with other mothers I visited.

"Well now, where's my manners? Come sit over here." She pointed to a chair across the room and sat down nearby.

When we were both seated, with my black book unopened in my lap, I asked Mrs. Rayburn, "How long have you been home from the hospital?"

"It's been three months this time. I just keep hoping and praying to the good Lord that I won't never have to go back to that place. They keep telling me I have to take my medicine so's I can stay home. I was so scared this time when they put those pads on my head and shocked me. I'm taking my medicine, now, even when I'm feeling good."

She seemed eager to talk, so I didn't interrupt her as she began talking about her family:

"I got three grown children—one's in college, one's in the Army and a daughter lives with her children down the street. She don't come to see me much. I got three children in school and the three little ones here with me every day—when I feel good. When I don't, Will—that's my husband—stays home to help out.

"He's a good man, works hard for the county when he can go to his job. He makes enough money to put food on the table and so we can have a good place to live. He and the school-aged children clean up and get the food cooking before they leave us in the morning."

Thinking the mother might not have much adult company, I asked, "Since you don't like to go out, do you have friends and family who come in to see you?"

The mother frowned as she spoke, "My daughter from down the street use to visit me. She'd come by every day and bring her babies for me to see. But, then she got mad at me for talking about my mama. She only comes now when Will can't be here and he asks her to come help out. She'll do anything he asks her to do. When she comes here, she says to me, 'Now, I don't want you talking that nonsense while I'm here.' So I keep quiet about my mama.

"People in the neighborhood walk by and look at the house, but just keep walking, turning away and holding their heads down. I've been away so much I don't have friends. I think they stay away from me because of the sickness I have. I reckon they're scared I'll do something to them. I feel kinda sad when they turn away, looking down and wandering off like they're not interested. Well, I do have my mama to talk to, and she never turns away; she comes everyday and we talk and talk."

I was relieved to hear this, for I was beginning to feel sorry for this mother of nine, housebound by her illness and by her feeling of rejection from neighbors and family. To encourage Mrs. Rayburn to continue to talk, I asked, "Does your mama live nearby?"

The woman shook her head, "Oh, no, Miss, she don't live close to me; she *passed* three years ago. That's when my sickness started. I miss her so much. At first, I'd just cry and cry. Nobody could make me feel any better. Will tried, but I couldn't make myself get up;

nothing mattered, not even the children. When I'd think about them, I'd know Will was taking care of everybody. People tried to shame me into getting out of bed, but I couldn't do it.

"Then, one day, my mama came to talk to me. When I told my family that she was here, they turned away like they didn't want to hear about it—no one would listen to me. They don't even want to hear what me and my mama talk about. Not even my Will listens when I want to tell him what we say to each other. He just acts like it don't matter; like she don't matter. It makes me sad that nobody will hear me, nobody will pay me no mind."

Mrs. Rayburn sat up and smiled, "Why, she's here now, sitting over there, smiling like she's glad you're here."

I was stunned into silence. The social work training I had received had not prepared me to deal with something like this. I was at a loss for words, trying to think how to respond. Then I remembered that my well-experienced supervisor had told me to use my instincts, my common sense when I was unsure what to do.

I knew that Mrs. Rayburn wanted someone to listen to her, and I knew I could be that someone. I could be the one person who would listen, who would not turn away. So I quietly asked, "What do you and your mama talk about?"

Mrs. Rayburn's body relaxed, she sank down in her chair and let out a deep sigh, as though she had waited a long time for this—for the chance to tell someone about talks with her mama.

"We talk about what a beautiful and peaceful place it is where she's gone. I tell her how much I miss her. She don't like seeing me have so many burdens here. She's upset when they send me off to that place where they shock me with the pads. Sometimes she reminds me how my children leave me when they're grown, and she says the others will do the same thing—except Connie who's slow. My mama wants me to go with her to that quiet place where I can lay my burdens down. She wants me to go with her now."

I was alarmed by this mother's remarks and quickly said, "Oh, you wouldn't want to do that. How would your family manage? What would little Connie do without you?"

"They'd manage, they always do when I go away, and they have Will. I talk and talk to my mama about Connie and what will happen to her when I go. I don't want her to be a burden to Will. So mama and me—we decided, if I go with her, I'll take Connie with me."

***

Several hours later, when I left the Rayburn house, the sky had darkened, and the birds were gone from the pond. My thoughts were on what I had done when I realized the mother was telling me that she was planning to kill herself and the youngest child. I learned that Mrs. Rayburn had been trying to tell someone about her plans for a long time, but no one would listen to her. No one wanted to hear her—maybe because they were afraid, and didn't know what to do. Or, maybe they just didn't take the woman seriously.

Well, now they would listen. I would make sure of that, and I would see that, this time, Mrs. Rayburn would get the right kind of help. I waited for Mr. Rayburn to come home from work, and then I went to a nearby phone to call my supervisor, Mrs. Nelson, for guidance. Tomorrow morning, I would make arrangements for the children to go into daycare when the father went to work. And the mother would have mental health treatment for her severe depression at a local facility, rather than have to be institutionalized many miles from her home. My department would provide other in-home services so the family could stay together.

I felt good about my day's work. Hey, maybe this *was* the place for me. I looked around as I turned my car back onto the road I was familiar with now, knowing that, in the months ahead, I would become more comfortable with all the areas of town where I could work with the children and their families. The birds were gone now, but they would be back, as would I. End

Novella

SECRETS IN A SMALL
SOUTHERN TOWN: A MYSTERY

CHAPTER 1

"Tim, can you come home soon? And can you take a few days off from work? The old man has died and Aunt Maude has asked me to come to Hamlin* right away.

"Oh God, I thought he'd live to be a hundred. She said there are rumors about someone causing his death, and she says she needs us. Otherwise, she'd never ask me to go back down there. She's asking us both to come. Will you go with me?"

*Fictional town is named for the German town about the Pied Piper of Hamlin who led the rats out, and then led the town's children out. If interested, use a search engine online for the story.

Anna was breathless and sounded desperate; almost hysterical. She had caught Tim at the precinct office where he was working late. He had never heard her sound so upset in all their years together.

Without asking any questions, he said, "I'll be there in an hour, try to get us on an early flight tomorrow."

They arrived in Hamlin at midday. The narrow sidewalks were empty except for a few people walking by. Nothing like the Chicago suburb they lived in where people were rushing by on their lunch hour to get errands done before they returned to work.

"Nothing has changed here since I left it years ago," Anna said as she stepped from the air-conditioned rental car they had picked up at the Birmingham airport. They moved from the car to the sizzling-hot sidewalk, into the sultry southern heat of the noonday sun.

"Why did I agree to come here for Lloyd's funeral, knowing it would be such an uncomfortably, hot, humid and miserable time in July?" she asked Tim as they watched the few people on the street slowly moving by. "I'd never have done this for anyone but Aunt Maude."

One of the people strolling by gave Anna and Tim a brief glance when she saw them watching her, and nodded as if to acknowledge them as she passed on by. She was dressed in cut-off jean short-shorts and a skimpy halter-top, had an earring tucked in her navel and three climbing up each earlobe. The colorful tattoo on her right leg encircled her ankle and meandered up her leg as though it was growing like a weed that was neglected and would continue up her body until it covered her like the kudzu in the South that takes over during the summer months.

Anna smiled at the girl as she passed them, and then whispered to Tim, "Well, some things have changed, for goodness sake! When I first came to this town with my mother, a well-meaning cousin warned me that a lady would only go downtown to the grocery store wearing a dress—no slacks and, God forbid, no shorts—and I was a mere child then."

Tim laughed as he envisioned Anna decked out in a dress for her frequent trips to the supermarket and health food shops near their home outside Chicago. Anna had moved there to work as a journalist for a small newspaper after graduating with honors from a mid-western college. She had met Tim, a police detective, while on assignment about the murder of a man who was leading two separate lives, complete with two families living only a few miles apart.

Anna joined him in laughter as she said to him, "Lloyd probably thought to his dying day, that dresses and gloves should still be proper attire in Hamlin, even though he never saw anyone dressed like that except in old movies or reruns of 'Leave It to Beaver.'"

"I suppose towns have many faces just like people do," Tim said as he pointed to a small café across the street. "Let's get some lunch there at the Country Cafe, some good southern cooking, like we had when your mother came to live with us. And maybe we'll see some characters that fit our expectations of this little Southern town, not like the tattooed lady we just saw."

The cold blast of air from the café hit them as they stepped through the door. The small room was packed and all the tables and booths were filled. "Guess we got here at the busiest time," Tim whispered to Anna as he looked around. "But, I'm not disappointed in the character of the room. Look at all the overalls and bushy beards, and every man has a cap on while he's eating. Wonder if they wear the caps to bed at night?"

Anna laughed, "No, probably not often, that's one of the times they take them off. Also, they don't wear them in the church. They look like different people when they go to church. You'll see tomorrow at the funeral."

Finally, a waitress who looked to be about 70 years old, wearing worn bedroom slippers, shuffled over and led them to a table. "Welcome to the Country Cafe. Sorry you had to wait so long, we're extra busy today and it's the factory's lunchtime. My name's Sadie. What can I get you to drink? Some sweet tea?" With lemon?"

As they sipped their tea, they ordered the luncheon special: chicken-fried pork chops, mashed potatoes and cream gravy, collards, sliced tomatoes, corn bread, and more sweetened ice tea. (recipes at end of the story).

Anna continued talking about the old man, "I've told you about his many idiosyncratic thoughts and actions, and his obsession with the television—his escape to the outside world. The television was always on when I called him every month."

Sadie brought their steaming plates of food and then refilled their ice-tea glasses. When she left, Tim asked, "Now, tell me again why you had to talk to him *every* month--and what *is* this *green stuff*?" Tim used his fork to poke at the collards on his plate.

"Well, I had promised Mother that I'd stay in touch with him like she did after she moved in with you and me. Just before she died five years ago, she said it was important to her for me to stay in touch with him—'family does that for each other,' she'd say. So I've done it for her, not him. I didn't question her; I just knew she wanted me to do it, so I did.

"And, that *green stuff* is a fragrant staple of the South—soul food," Anna said laughing as she sprinkled pepper sauce from a bottle of little green peppers found on each table in the restaurant. She then took a big bite of collards as Tim watched her.

She continued talking as they ate, "I'd call sometimes when his favorite show was on—*Wheel of Fortune*—which I quickly found out about when I made the mistake of calling during the time the game show was on. He didn't actually tell me that it was a bad time, but he would comment on something that was happening on the show rather than on my conversation with him, 'Now, why didn't he pick a vowel, so's he'd have more letters to work on?' he'd ask."

Tim shook his head, "Anna, I can't imagine that you didn't hang up on him."

"How could I? My mother was such a patient person and I was doing this for her, remember? Besides, he would sometimes give me new information about my mother and her family that I wouldn't have known if I hadn't called him. I would ask him questions about the family and he could talk for hours about them. I think that was his favorite thing to do, that is, if he was not engrossed in the game shows.

"Usually his questions to me were always the same at the beginning of the conversation: Are you going to church and are you reading your Bible? I always answered that I was doing both; then he'd begin talking, first, about his health which was good even though he was heading toward the 90-year mark, and then about the past, when he was a young man and free to roam the world. Mostly, he talked about his early years in Hamlin, the small Southern town he returned to after his adventures out West. I've seen pictures of him as a young man; he was handsome—tall and slim, standing by his sports car. He called it a *roadster,* saying it was the first one in the county and the girls liked to ride with him.

"He hated being old and usually commented on his age and the problems aging brings, like being stooped over and not being able to drive himself around town anymore. In his later years, he paid his good friend, Jack, to bring 'dinner' to him (lunch from the Country Cafe), and to eat with him. He would have Jack take him places in Lloyd's big Buick.

"I seldom had to say much since he loved to talk about himself. I might ask a question to get him started, and then he was *off and running*, with opinions about everything he discussed. He especially liked to talk about family matters—heritage and the family name. He was very proud of his family—his parents, aunts and uncles, his brother and sister, and all his cousins. He had one nephew, Dan, only child of his brother, Doc, and one niece, Selena, only child of his sister, Helen.

"He liked to brag about all the many relatives and townspeople he had helped financially, and he was forever telling different people that he had them in his will, possibly to keep them *beholden* to him. I'm expecting to see many people at his funeral—the people who went to him for handouts when there was 'a little money trouble' and the people who expect to benefit financially from his death.

Tim ordered warm peach cobbler with vanilla ice cream for them to share, and, then after the waitress left, he asked, "Do you expect to be in the will?"

"If so, I don't expect to get money. He might leave me some pictures of the family, especially since I've told him that I want to write a book about the family and would like pictures to add to the book. Even though both of his wives are dead, there are still plenty of family and friends who've stayed very close to him so he won't forget them," she said with a bit of sarcasm.

"Did he ever say he'd give you the pictures?"

"Well, no, but that was the way he was—he had a streak of meanness. He liked to control people and knew he could if he knew someone wanted or needed something from him. He had been married twice, but no children had been born to these unions, probably because he waited to marry until he was past middle age, and then married older women well past childbearing age.

"I wonder if it ever concerned him that he had no children to carry on his name. He never discussed it with me, of course, and I wouldn't ask him about something so personal. Some things I knew not to mention, like why did his second wife, Rose, leave him after living only a few years with him. He had dismissed her absence by saying she was not well and he certainly couldn't take care of her, so she went back home to Tennessee to have her family take care of her.

"After she left and later died, I heard from a cousin that he removed her picture and returned his first wife's picture to *the honored place* on the television set. After that, he spoke only of Belle, as though Rose had never existed. He made Belle out to be a saint, although he'd never said kind things about her or to her while she was alive.

"I don't think I ever mentioned to you that both wives told my cousins of his verbal cruelty to them. The hatefulness he expressed toward the wives only occurred in the privacy of their home. He appeared to be a kind and generous man in public. He probably never knew that both wives did not keep his nastiness toward them a secret in the small town."

Tim appeared to be in deep thought as he rubbed his full stomach after eating so much food. "You know, isn't that the way it is sometimes? It's like some of the meanest, most despicable people put on a kind face in public, hoping others won't believe it if they hear the secrets that go on behind closed doors. Makes me wonder if there are other secrets he had that family never knew."

CHAPTER 2

After they finished lunch, Anna and Tim headed to the motel to cool off and to get dressed to meet some of the family and friends at the old man's house. Anna was eager to see the cousins with whom she corresponded by phone, e-mail and social media. The other relatives she heard of only when Lloyd talked about them when she called him. She was interested in seeing how they looked, and how they interacted with one another. But, she was most eager to see Aunt Maude, and to find out why it was so urgent that she and Tim be in Hamlin now.

As they dressed, Anna asked, "Have you ever thought about how funerals bring people together for a short time, to briefly tell each other about their lives and give up-to-date information about their families? They take pictures of each other in their best clothes, smile at the camera, as though they're at a family reunion. Frequently, it's the only time they see each other, so it *is* like a family reunion. They try to be on their best behavior, which is easy to do because their time together is brief.

"Although they mention the deceased in passing, the death of a family member is sometimes used mainly by extended family to keep up with what's going on with the living relatives. There really isn't enough time to get to know one another, except to learn about them from the filtered facts that they choose to share."

"Yeah," Tim said, "It's especially interesting to attend a funeral gathering when I'm investigating the murder of the deceased, and to wonder if somebody in the funeral home is the guilty party. It's amazing how many people look guilty or afraid when they learn I'm the detective investigating the murder of the deceased. And, even if they aren't the murderer, they have their opinions of who did it and are afraid they'll reveal it to me. Babe, will you straighten my collar?"

As Anna smoothed his collar and straightened his tie, she asked if he remembered Aunt Maude. In the South, as a gesture of respect, one speaks to or of their elders with a title and their first name or nickname—some use miss or mister if the older person is not a relative; aunt or uncle if the speakers are younger, or if a close relative is a senior citizen; and cousin for the rest of the adult relatives.

"Isn't Maude the one you talk about the most, even more than you talk about Lloyd? Of course, I've never met her, as you know. Always wanted to come here to see where you grew up, but there was no talking you into it, so I gave up asking. Figured you'd tell me when you're ready—about why you resisted coming here all these years."

"And I will—someday—maybe soon, now that we're here. You know, Aunt Maude is Mother's first cousin, like Lloyd was. The three of them grew up together, along with other relatives, here in this small farming community. All of them are dead now except for Maude. She's still a small, spritely, and engaging woman who lives alone as she always has; never marrying. She was one of the few women of her generation who went away to college from Hamlin. When she graduated with her master's degree, she returned home to work in the community as a social worker, and to claim all the town's children as her own, since she never married and never had children.

"She is loved by everyone, that is, everyone who has not met her wrath because they have been abusive or neglectful to children or other helpless people. She never excused the abusers for all the reasons used today: being abused themselves, mental limitations, alcohol or drugs, being influenced by seeing abuse on television or movies, the devil made them do it, nor any of the many other reasons she said lawyers can come up with to get people off the hook for abusing a helpless child. She would stand up in court and say, 'Those are the *reasons* they give for abuse, but, as adults, the abusers are still responsible for their actions, and need someone to get their attention by putting the screws to them to stop the abuse.' She believed she was that someone and took her role seriously for many years.

"Oh, she believed that counseling helped, but if the abusers wouldn't get help, Maude was always there to see that they weren't *comfortable* in their abusive role. As the social worker, she considered herself to be the crusader for children's rights long before there were many child advocates in the country.

"After she retired at the age of 75 from child welfare services, she continued to champion for children's rights, and is still considered to be a spokesperson for the helpless and homeless people throughout the state. She's become more active with elder rights now that she's older."

As they left for Lloyd's house only a short distance from the motel, Anna asked Tim, "Now that Lloyd's gone, who do you think will become the intermediary for the family? Maybe Maudine?"

"Who's to say that anyone will?" Tim shrugged as if to say 'What does it matter, anyway?' "If people want to be close, they can do it themselves, like you and your cousins do now--through social media, phone calls, messaging, and e-mail."

"You're right, of course." Anna said and then thought to herself that the cynical detective Tim may be right but she wondered if close family ties were only Lloyd's wish, or if his interest in heritage and desire for closeness was embraced by other family members.

CHAPTER 3

Anna spotted Maude the second they walked into Lloyd's house. The living room was filled with people and she could see through to the dining room where the table was piled high with dishes of food. Maude was putting plates and silverware on the end of the table as she talked to a large young woman holding a baby, who was standing by her.

Maude hurried over to hug Anna as soon as she saw her and turned to Tim and hugged him, too. "Thank you for coming now and humoring an old woman. I'm so glad to finally meet you, Tim. I've heard so much about you from Anna's mother, Liz, before she left here, and then, she'd tell me what a great son you were to her after she went to live with you up North." She turned back to include Anna, "Now, I want *y'all* to stay with me while you're here and I won't take no for an answer, do you hear me? I should have mentioned it on the phone; guess I was too upset. I've got plenty of room, and I want to have lots of time to talk to you about why I've asked you to come.

"Right now, I want you to meet some of your relatives who are here already. Some of the others won't get here until tomorrow—just before Lloyd's funeral. But, first, let's get you something to eat. Everybody's brought tons of food." She led them over to the table.

After they assured her that they couldn't eat anything else after the Country Cafe, Maude turned to the young woman they had seem her with when they came in. "This is Cindy, your cousin, Skip's wife. She took care of Lloyd this past year—cleaning his house, driving him to doctor appointments, and cooking for him."

Anna's first impression was of a very young woman, friendly and outgoing. She smiled at Cindy and then reached to touch the baby, a delightful little boy, about eight months old. "He's precious; do you think he'll let me hold him when he gets to know me?"

"Oh, yeah, sure, Beau's used to lots of people holding him. Everybody's crazy about him at the day care where I take him. They fight over getting to hold him." Cindy beamed as she thrust the baby at Anna and looked around. "What could be keeping Skip? I swear, he's never here when he's needed." She frowned as she looked around. "He's probably gone fishing when he knows this yard needs mowing today. He promised Uncle Lloyd that he'd take care of the house and yard, and keep everything looking good. She headed for the front door, leaving the baby with Anna, pulling a cell phone out of her pocket as she went.

Anna turned to Maude with a questioning look. Maude nodded toward Cindy, "She's not got the patience with Skip like all his kinfolk do. His mother died when he was a toddler, and everybody has always tried to make up for that tragedy by giving him everything he wants and excusing his behavior. Now, Cindy's different, she's like a bulldog—she keeps after him, gnawing at the bone 'til he either does what she wants or he'll go off fishing or hunting. Well, enough about that. There are others I want you to see. Let me go find them."

Tim had been standing by Anna, playing with the baby. "What was that all about? Do you get the idea that Maude doesn't care much for Skip or his wife, Cindy? I think we're going to hear more about those two. Oh, by the way, while Maude's gone, what do you think about us staying with her while we're here? She'll be able to tell you more about the family for the book you want to write, and you may be able to get some pictures from her in case Lloyd didn't leave any for you. It will give us more time with her to find out why she wanted us here."

"Yes, I think that's a good idea, and I want you to see her house. It's full of the most gorgeous antiques and paintings—from several generations of the family. Isn't she just the most delightful, straight-forward person you've ever met? I've missed her so much."

Tim nodded, "I can't imagine her putting up with any kind of foolishness from Lloyd, like the way he treated other people. I'll bet you that he never got away with treating her anyway but with respect."

"Well, sure, but remember, it was only the people who wanted something from him that he treated nasty—like his wives. Here comes Aunt Maude; looks like she's found some people she wants us to meet."

Maude had two women, one on each side of her, holding them by their arms. They looked so much alike, they had to be twins. Both were wearing silk print dresses, and were beautifully groomed, with every hair in place. They looked like they had just come from the same hairdresser. The only difference in the two of them was the looks on their faces.

"These are your first cousins, your Uncle John's twin girls. Guess you haven't seen them since you went off to college. Tim, this is Mary Ann and Maudine. Don't try to guess which is which; even I don't know all the time. They were both named for me—Maudine, here, and Mary Ann for my other name, Mary. People say they were named for my two personalities—cheerful and serious. Maudine is my cheerful self and I suppose you can guess that Mary there is the serious one."

Maudine, with a big grin on her face, spoke first, "Give me a hug, both of you. Tim, it's good to finally meet you. And, Anna, you are looking great. Looks like you are getting younger while I'm getting older. I had about decided you were never coming back down here, especially after your mother moved up North to live with you. When Aunt Maude told us you were coming for the funeral, I said, 'Nothing but Cousin Lloyd's death would bring her back.' I heard you plan to write a book about the family, and he sure had a lot of material you can use. Hope he left it to you. If I can help, just call me. Hey, give me that baby; it's my turn to hold him."

As Maudine took the baby, Mary Ann stepped forward with her hand outstretched toward Anna, "It's so good to see you again after all these years. And this is Tim," she said as she turned toward him with a Mona Lisa smile. Anna and Tim were both so struck by the different manners of the twins; they were speechless for a second.

Maude rescued them by saying, "After you meet some more people here, why don't you take your things over to the house? Anna, you remember where it is, don't you? It's not locked, so you can go in by the side door off the portico, and take the first bedroom upstairs on the right. I'll join you at the house soon, 'cause the twins are here to relieve me. Don't know what I'd do without them."

After they were introduced to some more family, friends, and neighbors, Anna waved toward the twins as Maude led them to the front door. Tim had been talking to Jack, a close friend of Lloyd's and the one who brought his food from the restaurant everyday and ate with him. When they got into the car, he said, "Jack was asking me some very interesting questions about my job; it appears to be more than a general interest in detective work. Wonder what Maude will know about the gossip that Lloyd's health went downhill rapidly over the past six months, and some people are suspicious."

"If that's the case, wouldn't law enforcement here be looking into it?"

"You'd think so. Let's find out more about these rumors before I check it out with the authorities. I believe Maude wanted us here to look into this. She'd know if there's anything to the talk, wouldn't she?"

CHAPTER 4

When they pulled into the driveway of Maude's colonial brick house, Tim gave a low whistle. "This is right out of the pages of *Gone with the Wind* on a smaller scale. And she lives here alone?"

"Yes; just wait 'til you see the inside." Anna jumped out of the car and grabbed a bag. "I can't wait to see it again."

Tim, with more bags, was right behind her as Anna went through the side door, into a large room lined with bookshelves and filled with leather furniture. Everything was sparkling from lemon-scented furniture polish, and the scent, mixed with book leather and potpourri, gave the room a feeling of cleanliness, serenity, and times long ago. They set their bags down and Tim sank into a wing-back leather chair and sighed, "I could settle down here and not leave for a few days. Why haven't you told me about this place before now?"

"The trouble with this wonderful house is that it's in a less-than-wonderful town. Come on, I want to show you around. We're in the library. When I was a child, I spent many afternoons here after school, and sometimes, all day during the summer. It's probably where I learned to love reading *and writing*. Aunt Maude encouraged me—and all the cousins—to use it, and we had the run of the place.

Tim, reluctantly, got up to follow her. Anna continued giving him the *guided tour*, "The next room is the dining room—look at this massive furniture. When I think of childhood meals, I envision the adults in this room around this table, and all the younger kids, giggling around other tables in the breakfast room, library, and sun porch. We all loved coming here."

Anna ran into the formal living room, eager to see it all, with Tim right behind her. "During the holidays, Aunt Maude had a huge Christmas tree in here, and all the young cousins came to help her decorate it. Afterwards, we'd have cookies and punch that Sukie, the cook had helped her make earlier. She was always there for us when we needed someone to talk to. Our parents didn't seem to mind that we went to her, because they knew she was there for them, too.

"When Mother and I moved here after my dad died, Aunt Maude took us in until we could get settled into our own place. I think she helped with finances until Mother got a job teaching school, and I'm sure there was no loan—just pay back if and when you can. My mother would say to people, 'You *can* go home again, if you've got a Cousin Maude in your life.'"

Anna and Tim stood silent, looking around. Anna was remembering those early years when she had first come here as a young girl. She had missed her dad so much, but over the years, when something would scare her, or something would happen that she didn't understand, she knew this house and Aunt Maude would be here for her.

Then, that awful nightmare happened and she never felt safe again. That's why she went away to college—to get as far away from Hamlin as she could. She vowed she'd never return here. Yet, here she was.

Her mother would visit her at college, and then came to live with her and Tim in her last years. Anna realized there had been enough time and distance to heal, so that her pain had lessened and she was no longer afraid when she thought about that bad period that happened many years ago. Now, it was just sadness that kept her from revealing the past to Tim. Maybe soon, she would be able to talk about it without tears, but not quite yet.

Before they could complete the tour of the house, Maude came in. "I see your bags are still downstairs. Let's have a *co-cola* and rest a while before we go off to visitation at the funeral home. Now, sit down and put your feet up while I get us something cold to drink."

Anna and Tim followed Maude into the kitchen. The room had been kept up-to-date with a French-door refrigerator and a huge gas stove. The cherry cabinets were gleaming. "Aunt Maude, the house looks wonderful, and is just as clean and fresh as it always was. How do you do it?"

As they prepared the drinks, Maude told her how difficult it is to get domestic help now that the garment plant is in town and pays more than the residents of Hamlin are willing to pay for domestic help—that is for most people. But, she was so generous to her housekeeper and gardener that she had no trouble keeping someone to help her take care of the large place. "I've had the same couple, Sukie and her husband, Cade, working for me for many years. And they are still going strong. I have to *make* them take time off."

When they were settled in their chairs in the library with their cold drinks, Tim asked Maude about the rumors of Lloyd's health going down rapidly, and the suspicions that someone had assisted him along to his death. Maude said that she had heard the same rumors and that's why she wanted them here—that and some other reasons. She told them that Lloyd had never mentioned to her of being suspicious of anyone or anything. "I know he'd have talked to me about it if he thought anyone was up to no good."

"What about an autopsy; has one been done?" Tim asked.

"Not likely, since Lloyd specifically stated that one *not* be performed. Besides, he had spent the last month of his life in a nursing home, so, if something like poison had been used earlier, it would be hard to trace."

Tim looked with surprise and consternation, first at Maude and then at Anna. He was stunned to hear that, even if Lloyd hadn't wanted an autopsy, one wasn't done because of the suspicions of foul play.

Maude, noticing his dismay, said, "Things are done a little differently here, Tim; there's not a lot of crime in this little town. Sheriff Taylor stays pretty busy, trying to keep up with people who still make moonshine. This is still a dry county, so it's easier and cheaper for some of our citizens to make their own rather than to have to drive to the next county to buy the hard stuff. Besides, they've been making it for generations. That's about the extent of crime here—that and a few teens who like to bust up the mailboxes, driving by and hitting them with a bat. There's some drug use with the young people, but Sheriff Taylor appears to be on top of it.

"You ought to go talk to the sheriff, Tim, you'll like him. Nobody ran against him in the last election because he's so popular. Lloyd liked him and both of us contributed financially to his campaign and have supported him throughout his career."

"I think I'll do that. Maybe tomorrow morning? Will that be a good time, before the funeral services?"

"Yes, I think that's a good idea. I especially wanted you here to give us an objective opinion. You know, there are some pretty vicious rumors going 'round that could destroy innocent people's lives. If after you look into this and find there's no foul play, people will settle down if you give an informal, professional opinion. You won't be stepping on any official's toes, and we'll get it out there for everyone to know. You won't be breaking any laws just giving us your opinion, will you?"

Tim spoke slowly, "No, however, I'd be more comfortable giving an opinion if I had autopsy results. Let me talk to the sheriff before I answer you."

"Well, the funeral's not until three; that'll give everybody who's coming, plenty of time for travel. And while you're talking to the sheriff I can bring Anna up-to-date on the family members who're coming in tomorrow. I've got pictures and memorabilia that Lloyd gave me for you, Anna. He wanted to make sure *you* got it when he was gone. He said you were the most interested member of the family for the materials he had, and he was so pleased that you were going to write the history for the generations to come. And there's a lot I need to tell you; after all, I did promise you the family story, and it's past the time to tell it all.

"Now, if you're ready, take your bags to your bedroom and have a little quiet time before we have a light supper and then head on over to the funeral home."

CHAPTER 5

Several hours later, Tim opened the double doors, and he, Anna, and Maude went into a large room at the funeral home filled with people milling around. The crowd was speaking in hushed tones, and many of them looked toward the large doors as the trio entered. Several of the people Anna and Tim had met at Lloyd's house earlier in the day waved at them, and Maudine and a man headed toward them immediately.

"Oh, Anna, baby, I'm so glad you're here. Maudine hugged Anna, nodded to Maude and Tim, and kept on talking without taking a breath. "This is Henry, my husband, Anna, you remember him. We were all in high school together. After I got back from nursing school, we got married and we've been together ever since. Henry's on the road a lot; he's a salesman."

Anna saw a middle-aged man, casually dressed in summer slacks and short-sleeved shirt, shaking Tim's hand. She could not connect him to the teenager she knew when they were in high school—that wild but sweet and gentle boy that Maudine had loved since grade school. They were so different from each other, and appeared to still be—Maudine boisterous, generous, and always well-meaning, yet quick to get on people's nerves due to her assertive manner, and Henry still the mild-mannered Southern gentleman. Anna gave him a hug as Maudine kept talking.

"Just sorry it took a death to get you back. E-mails and social media are fine, but no substitute for a good ole fashioned sit-down-and-talk fest. I can't wait for us to get together and have some reminiscing about all those years before you left for college up North. Hey, remember when we…"

"Maudine, please give these people a chance to meet and talk to some other folks," Mary Ann interrupted Maudine as she walked up holding a young man by the hand. "Hello, Anna, Tim. This is Skip, Uncle Lloyd's nephew. Anna, remember Dan? This is his grandson. He's lived here all his life."

Mary Ann pulled Skip forward and he nodded his head shyly at Anna. "Uncle Lloyd told me about you. Sometimes, I'd be there with him when you'd call. He said you're gonna write a story about the family." He turned to Tim, smiled and held out his hand, "Hi, good to meet ya."

Anna subtly studied Skip closely as he and Tim talked. *He doesn't look like the Dan I remember,* she thought. *He must favor his mother's side of the family. But, you'd know that baby I held today is his, an exact replica.* Anna was still in Hamlin when his mother died in a car accident. He was only three years old, so he probably doesn't remember her at all. Anna recalled some of the e-mails from Maudine telling her about all the hardships Skip has had. He moved back and forth between his dad's and maternal grandmother's homes. His mother's family has catered to him and spoiled him in every way, giving him everything he wanted within their power.

Since becoming an adult, he's had numerous jobs, each one usually acquired by some well-meaning relative for him, but, alas, short-lived. Seems no one has ever expected him to be like other adults—responsible, accountable—in the short time he has been one. He just keeps on trying out new employment, works for a few weeks or a few months, and then something happens to cause him to lose the job. Maudine said a lot of the relatives resent family members helping him out financially and never expecting him to pay them back. Some would say he's had it easy, aside from losing his mother at such an early age, of course. Well, maybe not easy, but perhaps, effortlessly. But Maudine has told me that he's such a sweet person with a warm smile, everybody likes him.

Anna was brought back from her thoughts by the sound of a loud noise as the double doors to the room flew open and hit a chair nearby. A tall, dark-haired woman walked in briskly and headed toward Maude. She looked neither right nor left, as though she only saw one person in the room. In a loud, chilling voice, she said, "Maude, what's this about my uncle's will being changed without my knowledge? You would know, because he tells, er, told you everything. Why would he make changes at the last minute without telling me? After all, I'm in charge."

"Selena," Maude said in a strangely, cold-sounding voice, "Have you just gotten here? I would guess you went to the lawyer's office before coming to the funeral home to see your uncle. Well, now, looks like you've found out what he did to see that you didn't get it all. Come on; let's go into a private room if you insist on talking here. Or, do you want to see your uncle first? No? Then, come on to this room over here." Maude turned to go without checking to see if Selena was following her.

The visibly angry woman glanced at the people in the group Maude had just left and quickly followed, closing the door behind her. Her loud voice could be heard, "Who got to him? Who talked him into making these changes? Dan's going to be as furious as I am."

"Lower your voice, Selena," Maude spoke softly as if to encourage the same from the loud, enraged person towering over her. "We don't need the entire town aware of your greediness, now do we?"

"Don't use those counseling techniques on me, Maude, remember, I've been there; probably more years in treatment than you know. So your tricks don't work on me."

Selena lowered her voice considerably when she said the word "treatment," and continued heatedly but quieter, "He promised me I'd get the house and all the contents as well as the money. He'd been trying to get Dan to move here since I couldn't, but when I told him Dan's wife didn't like him, he began changing his mind about leaving anything to Dan that she could benefit from. Then, he got mad at Dan because he was selling that farm; we blamed Dan's wife for that, too. It just made it easier for me."

"Don't you think Lloyd saw through you? I've often wondered if you have a conscience," Maude said sternly.

"Of course, I have a conscience, but it doesn't keep me from doing things to protect myself. It does, sometimes keep me from *enjoying* them. It's true that Dan's wife didn't like Lloyd, but not many people did. I just used her to get what I needed. He was so sensitive to what most people thought of him—you know that. Now, what caused him to give part of my inheritance away?"

"Selena, Selena, you really do see it as all yours, don't you? Well, I think some things are beyond your control. Maybe Dan, for whatever reason, didn't feel the need to set Lloyd straight about you, but other people in this town felt Dan's side of the family should benefit from family money. Since Skip was here and appeared to be in need, and Lloyd needed him, they both helped each other to get what they wanted."

"But, that's not how I meant it to go down," Selena whined. "Cindy and I had it worked out—we'd both work on Lloyd and let him know we cared about him, and show him how others didn't. I'd then see that she and Skip would get some money. But he's left them the house *and* money. God, how could he do this after all my work?" She whirled and hit the back of a chair, sending it across the room.

"Looks like Cindy's not as stupid and naïve as you thought. Maybe, she had her own plans and played you for a sucker. She's the one you need to talk to. I've just been an observer."

"Oh, sure you are. Just a sweet little southern lady. Well, I'll get to the bottom of this, and I'm sure I'll find your doings somewhere down there. Well, I *will* get the rest of the money *and* that house back or at the least the contents, one way or the other." Selena turned and walked out of the room and straight out of the building without looking at anyone.

Maude returned to the group, shaking her head. "When you're ready, let's head on home. It's been a long day for all of us, and I want to tell Anna and Tim some things before bedtime. We'll see all of you at the funeral here tomorrow at three o'clock."

CHAPTER 6

When they got back to Maude's house, Tim made coffee and they sat in the library talking long into the night. Anna was concerned that Selena had upset the 90-year-old lady, but Maude was apparently unfazed by the earlier performance at the funeral home. She brushed it off by saying, "My skin's a lot thicker than Selena can penetrate. Besides, I was prepared for such a display 'cause I've seen Selena have 'hissy fits' when she didn't get her way."

Tonight Maude wanted to tell them about the family. "Well, Missy, guess you've already seen some of what this family is about. Seems where money is concerned there's no honor among the greedy ones. I was afraid of this, but Lloyd wouldn't listen. When he'd get a mad on, he didn't think rationally. He'd changed that will many times when he'd get angry at one family member or another. Looks like he never rectified it this time when he got mad and Dan's the loser. Many a time I'd see him change it when Selena would anger him, but she had a way of getting back on his good side. I teased him once by saying, 'She must have blackmailed you.' He didn't like it so I never said anything about *that* again.

"Anyway, where shall I start? What do you want? I have the pictures and books you'll need to pull the history together. Lloyd gave them to me so you'd be sure to get the materials. We'll probably have another bout with Selena about it, but if you're able to deal with her, we'll be okay. She's always hard to deal with so I leave her alone.

"If you want, I'll tell you a little of what it was like growing up here in the South back in the early part of the 20th century. If we were poor, we didn't know it. When one family had a bad crop, other families pitched in to help them, especially kinfolk. And the storekeepers would give credit to the families in need so they'd have food for themselves and feed for the livestock. Probably was not like that everywhere, but here in Hamlin that was the rule. We were like one big family.

"Our entertainment was each other—adults sitting on the open front porch most spring, summer, and fall nights and the children running around in the yard playing 'hide-n-seek' and catching lightning bugs. We'd put the bugs in a glass Mason jar with holes punched in the top for air, and then use the jar of bugs like a flash light. In the winter, the adults sat by the roaring fire in the fireplace while the children made popcorn and told ghost stories or read books in our library.

"Anna, your mother and her brother, and Lloyd and his sister and brother would come over to our place with their parents many an evening for supper and visiting afterwards. I loved it since I didn't have any siblings. They were all like my sisters and brothers, and Liz and Lloyd were my favorites. We grew up real close because we were the same age and in the same grade at school. We told each other *everything* and swore each other to secrecy about many things. To this day, there are things I've never told anyone—ever.

Maude talked late into the night and Anna had her tape recorder going, numbering and labeling each CD as it ended. Maude stopped only to answer their questions, patient with the interruptions. Tim had many questions to ask about the South, and Anna wanted to get more detail about the personalities of some of the characters she had heard about through the years.

At midnight, Tim went to bed, assured that Anna would continue to record Maude's narrative. When Maude went up to her room to change to her gown and robe, Anna followed with her recorder. "Aunt Maude, when are you going to tell me about your own life? What was it like leaving here, going away to college and then returning to this town?"

"Well, Sweetie, I didn't have the bad experience with this town that you had, and I always felt it was my place to return here to protect the innocent. I've always felt bad that you had those people abusing you—*the rats*—and I was not able to get them punished. And then to have the town not support you—well, things were different back then and the townspeople had trouble believing that such 'upstanding' citizens would do something so horrible to children.

"You may not know this, but that's when I left the job I had at the time and became a child's advocate for the county, and later for the state. I was able to get laws implemented that helped children who had been abused and to get perpetrators punished and sent away. I was also, with the help of many good citizens, able to have counseling made available for abused children. Because you suffered, and I wasn't able to help you as much as I wanted to, I became more involved in children's rights, and, now, many children are helped.

"Are you okay, Anna Baby? Please don't cry; it's been a long, long time ago, and those terrible people have been dead for many years."

Anna had only a few tears. "At first, I thought it would get better when they died; but, because I was so angry at so many people here, I decided that all of them had to die before I'd be okay. Then, when I'd been away for many years, and I matured somewhat, I figured they weren't hurting over it, only I was. I decided that I wouldn't let those depraved creatures continue to hurt me. I haven't told Tim; I don't know why. But I'll tell him soon—soon, when this is all over."

Maude told Anna more about the years before she left for college, then she stopped, looked at Anna as though she was trying to decide if she could continue with this. "What I'm going to tell you now needs to be told. Few people in Hamlin know this, but now that Lloyd's gone…he told me that once he's gone, he wants it told. He said he's suffered so much over this and it has alienated him from being close to others. He thinks times have changed, and now people are more accepting of others who are different from themselves. He wants his story told.

"So, I am compelled to make it a part of this family's story. It was his life and it affected everything he ever did. He confided in me when he was very young and didn't know what was happening to him."

Anna remained silent, waiting. She looked over at the recorder to make sure it was running. She had a strong feeling that this was going to be major.

Finally, after a long silence, Maude continued, "Lloyd was *gay*. When he was a boy, he didn't understand his feelings. There was no one to talk to about it except me, and I sure couldn't comprehend it, so I was no help except as a listening ear, and one who would keep his secret. As he got older, he would date the girls around here, so no one was suspicious. In those days, a man was considered to be 'a gentleman' who 'respected' women by not putting the moves on them.

"When all our friends and cousins were going off to college or working here in Hamlin and starting their own families, Lloyd decided to head out West. He took some courses at a technical school, and worked out there for many years. He finally returned to Hamlin to live with his aging parents when he was in his forties. He didn't confide in me after his return; kind of kept his distance.

"In fact, when he secretly married *an old-maid schoolteacher* from a nearby town, I learned of it when they finally told his family and the townspeople. I only guess that they kept it a secret for so long because of Lloyd's fear of his mother's wrath when she found out about it.

He had always been a mama's boy, and continued to be so after his marriage to Belle.

"The newlyweds built a house near his parents, and after his father's death, he spent more time with his mother than he did with his wife. There was no love lost between those two women, but he never got involved in their disputes. Both were strong women, but Belle was no match for his mother, Catherine. Why, even though his mother kept a portrait of one of his old girlfriends in the 'parlor' he never asked her to remove it, and, as much as Belle tried to get him to have the picture removed, it never happened.

"I was pleased when I learned he was married. I thought he'd gotten over his problem. Then, one day, about two years after their marriage, Belle came to my house to talk. She was always a busy person, keeping her house spotless, and helping out with her many relatives. But, she kept her distance from the townspeople, probably because she was such a talker, Lloyd didn't want her to get too close to an outsider and tell things about their life.

"The day she came to talk to me, I knew something was wrong. She never came over without other family or Lloyd with her. After we settled down with a cup of tea, she started right in. 'Maude,' she asked me, 'Did you know that we don't sleep together and never have?' I shook my head, speechless, and she continued on, 'He should have told me before we married, but to tell me on our wedding night was cruel. He told me that he needed someone to take care of him, to help him look respectful, and, in return, he'd take care of me—that I'd never want for anything. Well, he's kept that promise. I do have all the material things I want and a nice house; but I'm so lonely.' She began to cry. 'He has spells where he's so angry. Seems like it's at the world and I'll ask him what I've done that makes him yell at me, but he wouldn't say; he'll just be nasty when I ask.'

"I don't know if Belle ever guessed about Lloyd, but I knew then that he hadn't gotten over his problem. Of course, now I know being homosexual is not something one *gets over*. Once, after Belle had confided in me, I was checking criminal records for a potential employee as a part of my job, and on an impulse, I investigated Lloyd's record for when he was out West. Sure 'nuff, he had been arrested several times for solicitation.

When I asked him about it, he was furious. 'Why'd you nose into my business anyway?' He asked me heatedly. I apologized profusely, and because he had known how sympathetic I had been when we were young, he cooled off. He explained the problem he had out West was getting to meet people like himself. In those days, there were no gay bars or internet, and the only avenue for encounters was in places like the park. The public frowned on that practice, so routinely, on weekends, gays were picked up by the police and had to post bond to get out of jail to be back on their jobs by Monday morning.

"He finally got tired of it, and wanted a different life, so he came home, got married, and started his life over."

Anna sat quietly, "How sad. Who would have thought it? I knew from my cousins that both Belle and Rose were unhappy in their marriages to Lloyd, and figured he had to be unhappy if he was so mean to them, but I never suspected that he was gay."

Maude got up and stretched, "Let's get some sleep now, and tomorrow, we'll talk some more after the funeral. It'll be another full day with more family to meet. I know that Richard, Dan's son is coming, and you'll want to talk to him. He's very much interested in genealogy and he and Lloyd had many long talks about family matters."

Anna went to bed, but lay awake thinking about Lloyd and the many faces people have—the one they show to the world, the one they show to family; and, sometimes a secret one they don't want either family or friends to know about.

CHAPTER 7

When Anna awoke the next morning and looked at the clock, she was surprised to see how late it was. As she went downstairs, she heard voices in the kitchen where she found Tim drinking coffee and talking to a dark-skinned woman.

"Sukie, I can't believe it's you; it's been such a long time and you're still around here." As Anna hugged her, a black man walked in the back door carrying a big basket of tomatoes from the garden. "Cade, it's so great to see both of you and so comforting to know you're still around taking care of Aunt Maude." He smiled and nodded at both Anna and Tim as he set the basket on the counter.

Sukie said, "Now, Miz Anna, you know we wouldn't never leave her alone, not after all she's done for us. Tell me how you want your eggs; we've got ham and red-eye gravy, biscuits, and grits, of course."

As Anna declined eggs but requested a plateful of all the rest, Tim said: "That's the most amazing thing to watch Sukie make those biscuits, using that oblong, wooden bowl full of flour; and producing those lighter-than-light breads. It's an art; and, then, to bite into one is a culinary treat."

Sukie looked at him as though he was speaking another language. "Well, nobody's never put words like that to my plain cooking, but iffen you likes that, wait'll you try my Lane Cake. People tells me it melts in yo mouth. It's just the way my mama taught me to cook, so I been eatin' that way all my life. 'Course, when I was growin' up, Lane Cake was a special treat kept back just for Christmas time. Miz Maude done told me to fix one while you here, 'cause it be Miz Anna's favorite."

As Tim put down his empty coffee cup, he kissed the top of Anna's head, "I'm heading out to see the sheriff; have an appointment in a few minutes. See you back here soon." Anna waved him off as she bit into the delectable biscuit that she had just dipped into the red-eye gravy. She thought about how Sukie would be cooking for many hours, and seemed to love doing it.

Anna could imagine how fat she'd get if she ate like this on a regular basis. *But, Maude isn't overweight, so I guess if you're used to it and pace yourself, you can maintain a reasonable balance. Well, I'm not thinking about that since we're only here for a few days. Besides, what's that saying of the writer, Erma Bombeck? "Seize the moment. Remember all those women on the Titanic who waved off the dessert cart."*

~~~

As Tim walked into the downtown law enforcement office for his scheduled appointment, he was greeted by Sheriff Taylor who was leaning against the door frame, a tall, rangy, red-haired man, neatly dressed in his uniform with the pants tucked into cowboy boots.

"Welcome to our station, Detective, we're proud to have you visit us while you're here." His amiable manner, a wide grin, and a slow, easy accent made Tim feel welcomed, and gave him the surreal feeling that he was on the set of *The Andy Griffith Show* or *Mayberry RFD*. He expected a Barney-type deputy to swagger through the door at any moment.

What a difference this place is from my office in Chicago where phones are ringing, about a dozen detectives are interviewing victims, suspects, and witnesses to crimes, and the loud sounds of computer keyboards pounding out reports. If Maude is correct, this place is different. Would this sheriff even know how to go about investigating to see if a murder has been committed? Well, that's why she wanted me here; she doesn't think so. So, go slow, Tim thought to himself as he shook the grinning officer's hand.

"Thanks for your welcome. Thought I'd check with you concerning those homicide rumors about my wife's cousin, Lloyd Banks."

"Aw, those kinda rumors get started in a small place like this 'cause our folks don't have a lot to talk about crime-wise, and anytime there's somethin' new, it spreads like wildfire. It'll die down after 'while, when they git somethin' new to gossip about. Now, Miss Maude is worrin' about nothin' and I don't want her to bother herself about that hearsay."

"Sheriff, I'm not trying to tell you how to run your office, but, if there's any kind of suspicion, an autopsy needs to be done now, before he's buried. It'll be a lot more trouble and expense to have to exhume him if evidence is discovered later."

When the sheriff saw how serious Tim was, he stood up straight from leaning against the wall, turned and headed into his office. "Come on in here and tell me what you've heard," he said pleasantly as he closed the door after Tim walked in. They were in there for an hour. When the door opened again, they shook hands and then Tim headed for his car as he dialed his cell phone.

When he got Anna on the phone, he said, "I'm headed for the funeral home where the sheriff plans to meet me with a court order for the autopsy. He doesn't want any trouble later, so he's proceeding cautiously. The funeral may be delayed for a few hours, or not, so prepare Maude. I'll see you when it's over."

~~~

Maude stood at the front door where she had gone when she heard a car door slam. "Come in, Richard, I'm so glad you could come, and I want you to stay with me while you're here." She had to stretch up high to hug him. "I swear I believe you're taller than Dan, and more handsome, if that's possible."

As he bent over to embrace her, he lightheartedly said with a grin, "Well, what can I say?" Then, his tone changed, "Sorry Dad isn't coming; he was just here when Uncle Lloyd went into the nursing home last month. So, he decided not to return for the funeral. But, I'm here to represent the family and pay my respects to my great-uncle. He was good to me—helping me pay my way to college and sending me money once in a while. We had good talks about family; I think he was proud that I was interested in genealogy like he was."

"He was, Rich, and talked about it a lot. Now, come on in and have some breakfast. We've got your favorites, as I remember, and I want you to meet your cousin, Anna. She's a writer and planning a book about the family. She's here for a few days, and you two have lots to talk about."

After introductions to Anna, and a big breakfast from Sukie, Richard headed over to the funeral home. As he went through the double doors, he saw Selena coming out of the room where the uncle's casket was. "Rich, where's Dan? I need to talk to him as soon as possible."

"And hello to you, too, Cuz. Dad's not coming."

She screamed out, "What do you mean, not coming? This is outrageous. If I can come all the way from California, he can make a little short trip from Florida. I have to talk to him immediately, and I mean, right now. I'm calling him. Come on over to Lloyd's house when you finish here. I might as well tell you what Lloyd's done since you're the only one who's bothered to come to the funeral." She stormed out of the building and Richard could hear the tires screech as she sped out of the parking lot.

Later, when Richard got to Lloyd's house, Selena had not calmed down at all. She'd had to leave a message on Dan's phone to call her, so she was ready to talk. "Rich, you'll not believe what he's done. He's left Dan's part of the money *and* the house to Skip. He had promised me he was leaving almost everything to me, and now, look what he's done."

Richard had trouble comprehending this big change. He had known all these years that the largest portion of the family money that Lloyd got from his own parents would pass down to the next generation, which was Selena and his dad Dan. That's how family money is generally willed.

"What are you saying? Skip gets my dad's inheritance and the house? He's skipped two generations, that's not even rational. And, what's this about him promising you almost everything? This is madness. The old man must have been senile; out of his mind. Or mislead by my nephew, Skip. I'll talk to you later about you thinking you were getting it all. My mom always said that's what you were up to when you lied to the old man about her not liking him."

Selena ignored what he was saying. "Please let me tell Dan what Lloyd has done. It's my place to do it as the executrix of the will."

"Only if you get to him before I do. You're as sorry and depraved as my mom has always said you were, and I don't put it past you to have caused this problem." He walked out of the door, slamming it after himself. He headed over to Skip's apartment.

CHAPTER 8

Before noon, Tim and the sheriff were in the office of the funeral-home director, Jeff Mims. They had the court order in hand, and were expecting some opposition due to the suddenness of the request and the imminent funeral. However, with a limited amount of information and a quick look at the court order, the director released the body to the sheriff. He then began planning for a funeral service without a body and with only a few particulars given to the audience. Because there was no graveside service planned, he believed he could pull it off with a closed-casket service at the church. He picked up the phone to call and prepare Selena and the minister.

"Hello," Selena called out in her loud voice as she lifted the phone from its cradle. "Oh, Jeff, is everything ready for the service?" She listened for a minute to his explanation and then interrupted him. "No, we will not do it that way at all. I can't fight a court order; but I can have a say about how the service is to be conducted." Her voice rose even higher, "Now, listen to me, this is what we're going to do, and I want you to follow it to the letter, or there will be trouble."

The sheriff had called Selena earlier and told her about the rumors surrounding Lloyd's death. She was not surprised since she had already heard of the gossip from Lloyd's friend, Jack. She told the sheriff that she wouldn't oppose an autopsy, and had been waiting for the call from the funeral-home director.

Why delay the inevitable when, in fact, she had guessed this might happen? She was cooperative about the autopsy because she didn't want any delays that could postpone the distribution of funds from the will. But, by God, she'd still have some control over her uncle's final service.

She had been waiting for this day for many years, more years than anyone would even guess. Her patience was tested many times when the old man, with a short fuse like her own, would rant and rave at her about her standard of living—the frivolous way she spent money. She still had plenty of capital left from her mother's estate, but she was always "pore mouthing" to Lloyd in order to get funds from him. He usually gave her the money she requested, but only after she had to endure one of his outbursts at her.

Most of the time she bit her tongue, knowing that the money he would eventually give her and would leave her in his will would more than pay for the verbal abuse she had to endure from him. But, sometimes, especially when he would call her at night when she'd had too much to drink she would blow up at him and tell him off—about the many people he had hurt and the people he had misled, including herself. She'd call him names, like "nasty old hypocrite" and "two-faced faggot."

Yes, she had lost her temper once and let him know that she was aware of his *lifestyle* while he lived out West. In anger, she would accuse him of continuing that lifestyle in private now that he had returned to the South. She went too far that time; he cut her out of his will and, with glee, told her he was leaving everything to Dan. She couldn't let that happen, so she had apologized. She thought that biting her tongue was bad until she had to apologize many, many times.

Finally, when he wasn't moved by her apologies, she resorted to threats, to blackmail—she'd tell the world about his homosexuality if he didn't reinstate her in the will. He was livid at her and refused to talk to her for the longest time, but he finally realized that she had the proof to pull it off, and the gumption and maliciousness to follow through with the blackmail. In fact, he knew her well enough to know that she would enjoy telling the entire town about him if he didn't do what she requested; so he went to Lawyer Green's office and put her back in the will as before, with her and Dan sharing equally.

She couldn't stand the thought that anyone else would get some of that family money that they had no right to. After all, she had earned it— look at what she'd had to go through where people whispered about her behind her back. Worst than that was when they called her horrible names.

As a child, she used to beg her mother, Helen, to move away from here. Her mother could not begin to understand how cruel the children were to her at school, calling her a bastard and a half-breed. She knew they heard these things from their parents, and when she would ask her mother what they meant, she would only shrug and say they were just being mean. Helen worked in a large town about an hour from Hamlin, and kept to herself when she was not with family, so she didn't have to tolerate the distain of the townspeople.

Selena's teen years in Hamlin were extremely difficult. The only people she had to be with were the boys who were interested in her body, and because she was so lonely for companionship, she took their interest as friendship. By the time she was sixteen, she'd had two abortions, performed by a nurse's aide who lived off an unpaved road miles from the town. Both boys had denied being the fathers, but they helped her get the fetuses terminated and paid for them, and then ignored her afterwards.

That hurt each time, but she eventually got over it, saying that was okay because there were always plenty more guys waiting in line.

Her mother never knew about the pregnancies until Selena, in one of the many times she lost her temper, told Helen of the abortions and threatened to run away to find her father and live with him. That's when Helen, at long last, told her the story of her birth.

Selena had always been told that her mother and father met in college where her mother went to graduate school up North. Because her mother missed her parents, and wanted to raise Selena in a small town rather than the large city where she had been born, the two of them moved to Hamlin.

Selena never saw her father, and her mother said it was because he was angry that they left him. Her mother said the children at school only called her a half-breed because her father was from a country in Europe and was olive-skinned. Helen even had pictures of a dark-haired man she said was Selena's father and Selena did seem to favor him.

After her mother died, Selena found a letter in the safe-deposit box at the bank. That's when she learned that her mother was never married and that her father had been a student in graduate school with her. When he graduated, he went back to his country in Africa, never knowing of Helen's pregnancy. She left school but stayed up North until after Selena's birth, then returned to her hometown to be near her parents and other relatives, saying that her husband had been killed in a car accident.

After Selena's disclosure about the babies she had aborted, her mother agreed to move and they left Hamlin. Selena despised this place and returned only once every few years to keep intact her relationship with Lloyd. She knew that Maude had been aware of her trials with the town's children and of her reputation as a teenager, and hated her for not shielding her from the *rats of Hamlin* like she did for other vulnerable children.

She lived as far away from this town as she could get but it wasn't far enough away to forget her roots. She'd had three bad marriages that were long over and good riddance to them all. She had told all three of the husbands that she could not have children, and never told them the truth. It was no big thing to her to not have children because she did not like nor want kids, anyway.

Well, now it was her turn. She thought she had convinced Lloyd to leave everything to her, but somebody had persuaded him to share it with, not Dan, but his grandson, Skip. Damn, she had done such a good job convincing Lloyd that Dan didn't need the money and didn't care about him enough to move to Hamlin. She should have done a better job of persuading Cindy that she'd take care of her and her child if things went as they had planned.

She knew Skip wasn't conniving, or was he? He seemed so gullible, so easily maneuvered by that wife of his. He seemed to be unfocused, so unaware of what was going on in the world around him. But, someone had orchestrated this and she had to find out who it was. It couldn't have been that stupid Cindy. She had seemed so in awe of Selena that it looked like she'd do whatever she was told. Selena had convinced Lloyd to hire Cindy to help him, and then had told Cindy to keep making negative remarks to Lloyd about Dan and his wife when she was working around the house; and to continue to tell Lloyd how much Selena cared about him. She had planned everything so carefully but it wasn't working out like she had arranged it. She had to get Cindy alone and find out where things went wrong.

CHAPTER 9

Rich found Skip's apartment easily as it was in one of only two apartment buildings in town. When he pulled into the parking lot, he saw Cindy coming out through the entrance.

When he called to her, she turned and said, "Oh, hi, Uncle Rich, Skip's expecting you. Just go on up to 201 and I'll be back soon with Beau. He's at daycare and Skip wants you to see him. He's really proud of the baby and loves to show him off."

Rich nodded at her as she got into her car and left. Rich wanted to see Skip alone so he hurried up the stairs. He was ready to talk turkey with the kid about the old man's changing of the will and to see what Skip would tell him about it. He always felt that Skip had respected him as his uncle and they had a good relationship as the boy was growing up. He wasn't sure if he had changed as an adult, and wondered how much influence his wife had on him in these past few years.

Skip answered Rich's knock on the door quickly, like he was waiting for him. After their quick greeting and hug, they sat down to talk. Rich knew he didn't have much private time before Cindy got back with the baby, so he got right to the main subject.

"Hey, Skip, what do you know about this change in the will? Selena tells me you've replaced my dad as beneficiary? What did Lloyd tell you about it?"

Skip looked right at his Uncle Rich, knowing this was going to be rough going. "Uncle Lloyd told me he was doing this for my boy, Beau. He said he had helped you go to college and he wanted to be sure Beau got his education, too. I never did well in school so I never had any thoughts of getting a college degree. But, I'm hoping Beau will get to go now that Uncle Lloyd has provided a way.

"He said that Granddad Dan had plenty of money now that he's sold that farmland, so he wanted to help me out. He told me not to tell anyone about the change in his will because he didn't want to deal with the angry relatives. He said he wanted to be gone when they learned about it, and said I would have to handle it, but it would be worth it because I'd have the money. He even gave me a copy of the will so I'd believe him, I guess. I've been carrying it around in my truck and I look at it often.

"I can't believe he did it, but he was pretty upset when Daddy Dan sold the farm. Uncle Lloyd was hoping he was moving back here and when he sold it, he knew that wasn't happening."

Rich just sat there and looked at Skip. He knew the old man had a terrible temper but he never expected him to be so angry that he'd do this. He'd heard about the many times he changed the will but would change it back when he cooled off. This time he didn't get a chance to cool off.

He asked Skip, "Did Cindy know he had changed the will and was going to leave you all that money?"

"Well, yes sir. She was real excited and clapped her hands and then said. 'It worked.' I asked her what she meant and she told me that she had kinda 'pore-mouthed' to Uncle Lloyd when she would be over at his house cleaning or driving him to appointments. She knew how important family was to him, so she would tell him how smart Little Beau is and how he just loves people so much so she wants the best for him and hopes we'll be able to send him to college and give him a good start. She took Beau by to see Uncle Lloyd once in a while so he could see how friendly the baby is. And my mom's relatives were always reminding me to go see him often now that he didn't have anybody to take care of him other than Cindy who went every day."

Skip, appearing nervous, kept talking until Rich finally asked him a tough question, "Did you ever think how unfair it was for you to take his money—money that had gone to him from family and should go on in succession down to the next generation? Did you think how he had skipped two generations to give it to you?" Before Skip could answer these questions, Rich asked him if he had ever considered telling anybody, like his grandfather, what the old man had done.

Skip was looking down at the floor during the questioning, but looked up when he answered Rich, "My mama's relatives I told said I would be stupid to tell anybody in the Banks family, so I just kept quiet. Anyway, I figured when he got over his mad he'd change it back so Daddy Dan would get it. I really did!"

"Well, I guess that didn't happen and now you've got to do the right thing and give it back to your grandfather," Rich said as he got up from the chair to leave. He was disgusted and had to get out of there before he said or did something he might regret.

Just at that moment, Cindy walked in carrying the cutest baby. When Rich saw Beau all the anger went out of him, and when Cindy thrust the smiling baby toward him saying, "Go see your Uncle Rich," he took him in his arms and couldn't say another word. He played with Little Beau a few minutes and then left without looking at Skip or even Cindy as he handed the baby back to her as he walked out.

Rich thought to himself, *I won't give up trying to get this straightened out, especially after he heard raving Selena say she was expecting to get all of it. Maybe the old man really was senile; sure seemed like it with those conniving relatives jumping at the opportunity to get their hand in the till.*

When he got in his car, he called Lloyd's lawyer to see if he could get an immediate appointment and went directly there when Ed Green told him to come on over. As he sat down his first question to the lawyer was, "When did my uncle make this last change to the will giving my nephew the majority of the money?"

Ed Green told him, "It was about a month ago, around the same time that Dan sold the farmland. Lloyd came in 'fit to be tied.' Said that nephew of his just didn't appreciate family property and he needed to get his attention. He especially didn't appreciate that he wasn't consulted about the land, and would have considered buying it himself to give to Skip who has stayed here in town when no one else did and now helps him out. I was always here for your uncle when he needed to get something off his chest. He would usually come back in to see me after he'd had a little time to think about it and then we'd reverse the latest change.

"Ed, do you think my uncle had become senile this past year? Could that be the cause of his erratic behavior?"

Ed leaned forward across his desk and said, "Not a chance, that man's brain was as good as ever. He just had that hair-trigger temper, always had it as far as I know. I used to try to talk to him about the changes he was always making and how much money it was costing him, but he wouldn't listen. Said if I wouldn't do it he'd get another lawyer who would. I gave up and never questioned him again. I think he liked the control he thought it gave him. Not that I'd say that to him, remembering that temper."

Rich learned that the will would be read an hour after the funeral. Selena was the executrix and got to decide the time. She claimed she had to leave town as did some of the other funeral-goers, who were probably beneficiaries of the will, too.

When Rich left the law office he headed back to Maude's to talk to her about this latest change and to see if she thought Lawyer Green was trustworthy, or if he was taking advantage of a senile old man.

Maude was already dressed for the funeral with her hat and gloves on a foyer table. She was in the dining room putting the finishing touches on the lunch table as she talked to a group of people. More out-of-town relatives had arrived while he was gone, so Rich was waylaid by them and couldn't talk to Maude. Wonderful smells were coming from the kitchen as Sukie presided over the stove, and many dishes of food already covered the tables in the dining and breakfast rooms—foods brought in by friends and neighbors.

Southerners know how to cook and they show their love, affection, and sympathy with food. There was barbequed pork; Brunswick stew; green bean casserole; broccoli-raisin salad; chicken and dressing; relish dishes filled with watermelon rind pickles and fresh veggie strips with ranch dip; homemade yeast rolls; and one full table of desserts: Texas Sheet Cake, Kentucky Derby Pie, Red Velvet Cake, Southern Chocolate Pound Cake, and Strawberry Cake. (recipes are at the end of this story)

With Maude's experienced people skills, she had everyone seated at various tables in the living areas and they were having a great time visiting with friends and relatives they didn't see often while they enjoyed the good food. Maude kept her eye on the clock, so no one would be late to the funeral of her cousin and good friend—the last one of her generation except for her.

~~~

Selena called Cindy's cell phone, "You need to come to Lloyd's house ASAP," and hung up. Cindy was there in 10 minutes, having left a sleepy baby with Skip.

Selena, dispensing with greetings as was her usual manner, said, "So how did you get Lloyd to leave you all that money and his house, too? I know you did it since Skip doesn't even know how to scheme. I thought we had an arrangement. You were to tell him how much I cared about him while running Dan and Susan down."

"Cindy kept her chin high as she stood up to Selena, saying, "I did that, a lot, and I also bragged on my child. I wanted Uncle Lloyd to know we were here for him, and we were—the only family who was. I had to nudge Skip to come over here to visit, but he came. I let Uncle Lloyd know how poor we were and he knew it, because he paid me a lot of money for keeping house for him and taking him places. He even bought Skip a fishing boat because he knew how much Skip loved to fish. We did things for Uncle Lloyd and he did things for us.

"Uncle Lloyd this and Uncle Lloyd that," Selena screamed, "That makes me sick, thinking how you fooled him with that *lovey-dovey* manner. You don't care a thing about him."

"That's not true. We do care about him. Everybody at church says how he bragged on us about how we helped him. I like to think we kept him from being lonely."

Selena yelled, "I can't believe he left this house and everything in it to the likes of you. I want the antiques that belong to my family and that I grew up with. If you give me a hassle about them, I'll make your lives miserable."

Cindy said, "Take whatever you want. I'm sure Skip won't mind. When are you leaving? When can you get the things you want? We're not moving in for two weeks."

Selena made a list of her wants, left it with Cindy, made arrangements for a mover, then she made plans to leave town after the reading of the will. After talking to Dan she decided there was no hope of getting all of the money nor the house. *Well, I tried*, she thought

CHAPTER 10

When Anna and Tim got to the church, people dressed in their "Sunday-best" were moving up the steps and into the vestibule. A few men had on ties and jackets, but because of the heat most of them were in short-sleeve shirts and dress slacks. As Anna had guessed, none of the men had their caps on. Some older women had hats and gloves, like Maude did but the younger adult women had on their nice dresses and shoes without stockings.

Anna nodded toward the people filing into the church, "See, Tim, the men are able to leave their caps at home. And have you noticed that there are no children? Wait, there's Skip and Cindy with Beau. That couple loves the attention they get when the baby is with them."

"Yes, and they also figure everyone knows about the change in the will and the people coming here today will want to see him; especially those from out of town who are only here for the funeral. That was a good call on Skip's part to bring him," Tim said.

"I'm sure some of Skip's relatives suggested it. Aunt Maude said he's had many advisors, even though he doesn't always listen to them. She thinks he did listen to them about staying close to Lloyd and that's why he's getting the big money. Maybe he'll learn from this and pay more attention to their advice."

Tim had been watching Anna carefully all day, wondering about her tenseness. He asked her a couple of times if she was doing okay, and now asked her if she would be alright with all these townspeople around.

She nodded yes and said, "With the people in this town you never know what's going to happen. I haven't trusted them since long before I went away, but most of the ones that bothered me the most have either died or moved away. If there are any left, I'm thinking they won't show up today since they know that Maude and I will be here. But," she repeated, "You never know what's going to happen."

Tim looked at her and held her hand, knowing now was not the time to say anything. After a few minutes they got out of the car and walked into the church. Tim took Anna's hand again as they went up the church steps and held it tight. Anna looked at him with grateful eyes; glad that he was by her side and aware of her feelings.

Music was playing as they went in and sat down in the marked-off family area. Selena sat on the first row along with Maude, Skip, the twins and their families. Rich was there, too, but sat apart from the others. Cindy stayed in the back in case Beau got restless, but right now he was having a good time with all new people playing with him.

When Pastor Johnson entered the room from the back of the church and sat in his church seat near the pulpit, the whispering ceased. The closed casket was on a stand with a picture of Lloyd on top, and on the floor in front of him were many floral arrangements spread around the casket. Although Lloyd's body was not in the casket, Selena had insisted that fact would not be divulged to the audience. She wanted them to think that he was there, and didn't think they needed to know he was off being autopsied while the service was in progress. No one involved in the arrangements was willing to cross her, so everything went as she wanted it.

After an announcement that there would be no graveside service, the minister followed Selena's directions to the letter. It was a speedy service since no one was asked to say anything about Lloyd. Selena just wanted this part over so she could get to the reading of the will. People gathered outside after the service, fanning themselves with the funeral programs, many wondering why they had come this long distance for such a brief time. However, this did give them more time to visit and they took advantage of it, some gossiping about the things they were hearing of the rumors surrounding Lloyd's death. And many of them were waiting the hour after the funeral for the reading of the will at Lawyer Green's office.

To Anna who was watching the people milling around outside, it reminded her of the scene after the hearing of the "Notorious Nine," the group of adults who ran the summer camp she attended all those many summers ago. She was remembering, *As they waited to hear from the Grand Jury about their alleged abuse of the fifty children who attended the camp, they didn't look any more concerned about the findings than these people today who are waiting for the will to be read. She realized now that those nine people knew they would not be prosecuted for the crimes to those children since the very people who were deciding their fate were their own friends and neighbors.*

It seemed simply that the Grand Jury did not, could not believe that the people they had grown up with and had gone to church and school with could do something so heinous to children. Aunt Maude tried to get them prosecuted but the Grand Jury, the lawyers, and the judge thought she was being naïve when the children told her what was happening to them. No one ever believed this could happen in their town of Hamlin. And then, when questioned, many of the children recanted what they had accused the adults of. But, at least it ended the nightmare she was living once it was out in the open, and after years of therapy for her and some of the other children, she was able to move on in her life.

She was always grateful that she knew she could go to Maude, who believed her and tried to help her and the others. Why, if it weren't for her, who knows if it would have ever ended before all those children were severely damaged.

"Where are you?" Tim asked, as he looked with her out of the church window overlooking the parking lot where some people still were standing, reluctant to leave.

"Oh, I was just remembering something that happened many years ago, and I'm realizing just talking about it isn't going to make it real again. I think that's been my fear all these years—that if I talked about it with you, it would all come back to haunt me."

Tim knew it was best to stay silent right now. They had to get through the reading of the will and he didn't want to make Anna more tense than she had been for most of the day. "Babe, you can talk about this later when we leave here. You've had enough drama for now, and still have to get through the rest of the day. Will you be okay to wait a few more hours?"

Anna laughed, expelling some of her tension, "Yes, it can wait a few more hours, but then you'll have to hear me talk about the worst thing that ever happened to me. Do you think you're ready for this?"

"You know I am; I've been willing to listen to this part of your life whenever you're ready to tell me." He wrapped her in his arms and gave her a big hug. "Let's leave here now, go by Maude's house for a cool drink and then go on to the law office. Are you ready?"

Anna took his arm as they left the church, squeezed it and said, "How did I get so lucky to find you? Was it in the stars? Were we destined to be together?"

As Tim helped her into the car, he answered her, "I like to think it was destiny. Why else would we have been at the same crime scene in the middle of a big city—you a young, innocent southern girl, just out of college; me a tough, experienced cop from the streets, wondering if I was ever going to meet the right kind of girl that I could take home to my mama. And, then there you were."

CHAPTER 11

Anna sat close up to Tim as they drove to the law office, thinking, *This man is so able to help me feel comfortable; he knows when to say the right thing that relaxes me. What if I had never chosen to go North to college and stay there after graduation to work there so I didn't have to go back to Hamlin? Finding Tim happened because of the rats of Hamlin. How could something so good come from something so bad? Well, there you go; it had to be destiny.* And her body let go of all the tension.

When Anna and Tim entered Ed Green's conference room at his law office, it was crowded with the same people they had just seen at Lloyd's funeral. Anna thought, *everybody who's here was at the funeral.* She was happy to see that none of the *Notorious Nine* were at either gathering. Most of them moved away from Hamlin after the grand jury findings were presented, back those many years ago, and her cousin, Maudine had told her that they never showed their sorry faces in town again.

Those who left had lost their jobs in town and went away to find new employment. The three who stayed in town were the older men who soon retired and they stayed out of sight for the most part. They were never the force and influence they had been before their exposure.

Selena was at Ed's desk talking to him, whispering for once. She turned to the people in the room saying, "I'm passing a legal pad around the room and want everyone's name, current address, phone number, and social security number. Hopefully, there'll be no challenge to the will to delay a quick disbursement of the funds. It's highly unlikely you could win even if you do challenge it, so keep that in mind if you're considering it." Ed had told Selena this and she spoke as though she had authority.

Maude was shaking her head slightly as she sat in a leather chair near Ed's desk. Ed himself interrupted Selena, something few people ever did, to say, "I'll handle those details about procedure. Thanks for your help, Selena. Let's get started now that everyone is present that I contacted."

After everyone was seated and quiet, Ed began, "This is the reading of The Last Will and Testament of Lloyd Rueben Banks, dated on May 29, 2008. If anyone here is in possession of a will of his which would be dated later than May 29, 2008, please present it now, or inform me of it before I continue." He sat, looking around the room for a minute. When no one spoke up, he then proceeded.

Anna was amazed at how many people the old man remembered in his will, even though she heard that he had told a lot of people that he planned to leave them money. However, a large portion of it went to Skip and Selena, with all his relatives of Dan, grand-nieces and nephews, and close cousins also getting a portion. Anna was surprised that Lloyd had remembered her, leaving her money to pursue the writing of the family book.

No one there acted surprised that Skip was replacing his grandfather as a main beneficiary, so word had spread quickly, but there was a sound of surprise when Skip also got Lloyd's house. Few knew that Dan, Skip's grandfather had suggested to Lloyd that he leave it to Skip since he was the last remaining close relative living in Hamlin and Dan didn't want Selena to get it. Dan had told Skip this, but he didn't know at that time Lloyd was also leaving the money to Skip. Dan knew Lloyd was angry at him for selling the farm without consulting him first.

However, Lloyd left Dan and his children more than they were expecting to get. And, although she didn't need the money he left to Maude, his "dearest friend and cousin," a bank account he had set up to cover all expenses for the care of the family burial plot, where the graves of his parents, his deceased wife, Belle, and other relatives were "resting." His good friend, Jack was named to take over the bank account and care of the plot when Maude was no longer able to. It was clear from his arrangements that he didn't think Skip would be responsible enough for something so dear to Lloyd's heart.

After receiving instructions on the disbursement of the funds, people left the office slowly, with a few standing around in the open spaces of the parking lot to discuss the details of the will they had just heard. Most of the out-of-towners left soon after for their trips home. After Anna had hugged many of those people and some townspeople, they got Maude into their rental car and headed back to her house.

As they rode away from the law office, Anna thought, *Finally, the funeral and reading of the will is done; now all we have to do is the autopsy and my telling Tim the Hamlin story about the Notorious Nine.*

We expect to be alone at Maude's for the first time since our first day here, so maybe we will have time to continue our discussion of Lloyd's sudden death and the rumors surrounding it; but not until Maude has rested.

She asked Tim who was driving, "When do you expect to get the autopsy results? I hope soon since we need to get home." She was riding in the back with Maude and holding her hand.

"Sheriff Taylor said that he'd put a rush on it since we can't stay long here, so we should have the preliminary results released to us within 24 hours, but the full results of an autopsy may take up to six weeks to prepare. We should be able to determine if he had been poisoned with the preliminary results.

Maude had been quiet on the ride home. Anna thought she looked tired, so she wanted to get her home to rest before they did any more talking. Maude leaned toward Tim, "I was surprised at how many people were talking about someone killing Lloyd. I'm hoping you will give an opinion, so we can stop all this talk and speculation. I never expected this amount of talk and I'm surprised at the different people the gossipers are targeting."

Tim turned the car into Maude's driveway, pulling up close to the portico. Anna said to Maude, "Let's let it rest a while so you can get a nap. You've probably been up since dawn and I know you've always been like the Energizer Bunny, 'just keeps on going and going,' but this has been difficult for you."

Maude didn't argue with Anna as she got out of the car, realizing Anna was right. So she agreed to go to her room for a while. Anna was frowning as she watched her go and said to Tim,

"It's just so hard to think that Aunt Maude won't always be here, handling everything for us. I've got to get her to slow down. Do you think we can get her to come home with us for a long rest, and to get her away from all this turmoil?"

Tim said, "We can try, but I don't expect she'll come right now until all this talk is settled. Let's both encourage her and then promise to come back down to get her when she's ready to come with us. I know you're worried about her, but no more pressure right now, okay?"

CHAPTER 12

Anna and Tim went to their room where they sat in chairs by the window. Anna asked Tim if he was ready to hear her story of long, long ago. He reached for her hand and told her he was and that he believed she was ready to tell him. He even suggested she record it as it was part of the story of her family she was planning to write about. She was quiet a moment while she thought about doing it—was she ready for that?

Quickly, she thought, I can do that—record it and if it felt right when it came time to write that chapter of her life, she'd have it ready to go. She got up to get her recorder and several discs in case it got lengthy with details.

She looked out of the window and began, "When I was 10 years old my daddy died. I was devastated and having a tough time. Mom wasn't much help because she was very close to him, too. We three were so close we didn't need anyone else. After he died, Mother called Aunt Maude often, and one of the times she called, Aunt Maude suggested that we think about returning to Hamlin. She said we could live with her until we were ready to go out on our own. She also offered financial help to us until Mother could get a job teaching school.

When Mother told me about the offer, she said she could do it if I thought I'd want to. We used to visit Hamlin about once a year before my dad died and it was always fun, so I told her, "Let's do it." Once school was out in June, we packed up, stored our furniture and moved to Hamlin.

"Aunt Maude made us feel right at home, feeding us good southern food, taking us to visit our relatives, and shopping in Columbus, the city close by. Her friends became our friends, too. And Mother had many friends from her childhood. Aunt Maude didn't need a reason for a party, so we had many impromptu get-togethers with lots of cousins and children close to my age. When school started in the fall, I wasn't scared in a new school because I already knew many of the students in my class from the summer parties.

Also, Mother had gotten a teaching job in the high school, so every day, when my class let out, I'd go next door to the high school where I'd wait for her to finish and we could go home together. Oh, I wish it had stayed that way!" Anna said with a break in her voice.

Tim took her hand again and asked her if she wanted to take a break, but now that she had gotten started she wanted to continue. So she shook her head and said, "We stayed with Aunt Maude until after Christmas and during the school break we moved to our own place. Mother was stronger by then so I felt more secure.

"It was the next summer when Aunt Maude's friend, Judge Larsen offered me a place at the summer camp he ran for the Hamlin children at a ranch he owned about three miles outside town. Aunt Maude said he had set up this camp for the children whose parents both worked or children who only had one parent. He had started it as a day camp, and stressed the safeness for the children, so few people said no to him. It was a big success and the children had a great time. He provided picnics, trips to the movies, passes to the circus when it came to Columbus, and bought a bus for everyone to ride together when they took the trips.

"I think it was the fourth year he had a big sign made: The Hamlin Children's Camp. He had 10 cabins built; each one could sleep 6 children and a counselor. Since it was so successful, he was able to set up a fund to make it free to all the children, and townspeople were happy to contribute to something that was so good for the children of Hamlin. So now, it was a camp where the children could stay all summer and parents didn't have to worry about their safety. This is the year I started going there.

"Mother didn't think she had anything to worry about; after all, it was run by the Judge and supported by the townspeople. What would she have to worry about? Even Aunt Maude thought it was a good place for me to go while Mother taught summer school.

"The parents were encouraged to visit often, and were happy to follow the strict scheduled times offered to visit, not wanting to interrupt the activities of the camp. Over the years, the Judge would only hire people he knew as camp counselors—no outsiders. Generally, it was Hamlin's young adults and college students out of classes for the summer.

"I had a good time those first years going there and made lots of friends. Mother and Aunt Maude came every weekend so I had that to look forward to. They were happy I was having such fun. My cousins didn't get to go because they didn't qualify—they had two parents. So I didn't get to see much of the twins during those summers.

"It was in my third year going to the camp, when I was 15 years old, that everything changed. By that time, more cabins had been built and there was now a large recreation building. Several of those newer cabins were built further out in the woods, near the lake, so they were isolated from the other cabins. The camp counselors who didn't sleep at the children's' cabins stayed there and the camp children didn't go there, or so I thought.

"One day two of the older girls, Julie and Denise, asked if I had ever been invited to go to Cabin 10. I said, 'No. I thought only the counselors were permitted there.' They looked at each other like they had a secret. Then Julie said 'You've been invited to attend a special party there tonight. Don't tell anyone; this is just for special people and if you tell you'll get into big trouble, okay?'

"I was curious, so I said yes. I can't believe how naïve I was! They said to be there at ten o'clock and I said, "That's after curfew!" They both laughed like I'd said something really funny and said 'Be there' as they walked away. Well, it was my first time to break a rule but I really wanted to go because they told me that Jimmy would be there and wanted to see me. He was the counselor I had a crush on but had never told a soul. Was it that obvious?

"I left my cabin that night all excited with anticipation. I never thought about what I was going to find; all I could think about was Jimmy. I knocked softly on the door and Denise let me in. I was surprised to see two girls I knew; they were two grades ahead of me so we weren't close friends but they were in my Sunday school class. They both looked away when I walked into the room.

"As I got settled on the couch, Jimmy came and sat down by me and said, 'I'm glad you came. We'll have fun so don't be afraid.' And we did have fun that night, talking for a few hours and getting to know each other. We were so into each other I didn't notice as the people in the room thinned out. When I saw there were few people in the room, I realized how late it was, so I jumped up and said I had to leave. I got back into my cabin and into my bed without waking anyone. I'd decided I'd say I had been to the bathhouse where the showers were if anyone asked.

"Because it had been so easy to go and come without anyone challenging me, I started going three or four nights a week. Jimmy and I got a lot closer and did some heavy petting, but I'd never go as far as he wanted to. Finally, when I continued to resist him, he said he wanted to show me a secret: We got up from the couch and went over to a large bookcase where Jimmy tipped a book forward and the bookcase moved to show an opening.

He led me through the opening and down some stairs to a cave-like room where the kids were making out. I was so embarrassed when I saw what they were doing that I turned my head and when I did I saw the Judge and some other adults watching the kids from a place higher up that looked like a box at a ballgame. They weren't looking at me, but then I saw that they were watching the other kids who were in some awful positions and doing some weird things that still embarrass me when I think about it.

I saw cameras on two walls that were on and it looked like they were filming the kids as they were performing the sex acts. They had to know they were being recorded; the cameras and lights were so bright.

"I can't do this," I said as I turned and quickly went back the way we had come. I was crying by now, so afraid I'd have to do what the others were doing since I was in this cabin. Jimmy had followed me out of the cave and watched me leave the cabin, not saying a word. He ignored me from then on and I was glad 'cause I didn't want to think about what we had been doing.

"I never went back to that cabin again and when I talked to my mother and then Aunt Maude about what I saw, they wanted me to repeat it to some social workers and lawyers from Birmingham, which I did. The Judge and his friends who were there that night denied what I said, and when I had to repeat it before the Grand Jury, they said I was making it up. Many of the kids who were there, at first, told what they were doing, but then got scared and recanted when the Grand Jury convened.

"Even though the Grand Jury saw the cabin and the cave inside, they acted like they believed the Judge when he told them I was a disturbed child who had lost her father and had recently moved here and was having a hard time adjusting. This was during the time the McMartin day-care child-abuse case trial was going on and those accusers and children were being discredited.

Members of the McMartin family, who operated a preschool in California, were charged with numerous acts of sexual abuse of children in their care in 1983. After six years of criminal trials, no convictions were obtained, and all charges were dropped in 1990.

"In the end no one in that case was found guilty and that's what happened in the Hamlin case. Even though I told them about the cameras, they were never found. The Judge said that was just some more of my creative lying.

"None of my friends would have anything to do with me after that because either they had been there, or, those who weren't, believed I had lied for attention and their parents didn't want them involved with someone so vindictive that she'd try to harm some people like the Judge and his friends who were just trying to help children.

"Even though there were no convictions, the Judge closed the summer camp and padlocks were put on all the gates and cabin doors. Later, the place was sold and became vacation cabin rentals after the Judge died. Most people involved with the cabins left town and never returned.

"The people of Hamlin didn't believe me and were furious at me, believing I was the cause of the camp closing. No one but my relatives would speak to me after that. Even my teachers were distant with me."

Anna's voice broke and tears rolled down her cheeks, "Why would they treat me like I was the one who did something wrong? I was very lonely and became a recluse when I wasn't in school. That's when I began spending more time in Aunt Maude's library. I felt safe because when Aunt Maude was at work, she made sure Sukie was always at the house for me.

"It was never the same after that and so Mother didn't object when I wanted to go North for college and then stayed there after I graduated, never even coming back here for a visit."

Then Anna was quiet and so was Tim. It seemed to Tim that her sadness was about her friends abandoning her and townspeople not believing her, rather than her participation in the episodes with Jimmy. He asked, "Did you feel guilty about any of it because *you know* you were not to blame?"

"No; at first I cried a lot because I had lost my friends, my fun, and even Jimmy; but then the sadness turned to anger that people blamed me and not the Judge and his friends. I know I'll always be upset about the way the townspeople reacted, but the last few days have shown me that I'm over it--finally."

CHAPTER 13

Anna and Tim found Maude in the kitchen making iced tea for them. "Were you able to rest any?" Anna asked Maude.

"Yes, and I think we finally have time to talk about the reason I wanted Tim here. Let's take our tea into the library to talk. Maybe we won't have any interruptions."

Tim took the tea tray and Maude brought some of the Lane Cake Sukie had made earlier.

"Oh, that is so good and so rich," Anna said with her mouth full and her eyes closed. She took another bite as Maude began talking.

"What I'm about to tell you can never leave this room. You have to assure me that you won't tell anyone what I'm going to say. Please say you won't implicate anyone, no matter what I say." Anna and Tim both nodded but didn't speak, waiting for Maude's story.

She began talking, not waiting for them to speak, "Lloyd was getting feeble fast over the past few months before he went to the nursing home. He said he didn't want to spend his last days getting weaker and having to depend on the staff there to care for him. He was afraid of getting AIDS in his last years. He asked me if Henry, Maudine's husband, knew much about the drugs he sold. Henry has worked for the past ten years as a traveling salesman for a drug company out of Birmingham and New York.

"Lloyd said he had talked to his doctor about assisted suicide, but the doctor said he couldn't help him because of the Kevorkian case. Lloyd's doctor gave him a recording of Dr. Jack Kevorkian being interviewed by Mike Wallace on *60 Minutes* after the doctor got out of prison where he had spent *eight years* for assisting a neighbor of his, Tom Youk, in dying. Lloyd asked me to watch it with him.

"Tom Youk led an active life; he restored and raced vintage cars. But at the age of 50 he was diagnosed with Lou Gehrig's disease, a devastating, incurable illness that destroyed his muscles. He lost the use of his legs and then his arms. His family says he was in terrible pain, had trouble breathing and swallowing, and was choking on his own saliva. So they contacted Dr. K., who lived nearby, and he videotaped his first meeting with Tom.

"Trying to talk to Tom, Dr. K. learned how bad he was. He told Mike Wallace that Tom could barely make intelligible word and you could see him breathing, gasping, and leaning back every time he tried to talk. He couldn't utter more than a few syllables at a time because of the weak muscles. And he was terrified of choking!

"In that interview many years ago, Dr. K. told *60 Minutes* he had helped more than 100 people to die by having the patient pull the switch to start the lethal drugs flowing. Tom Youk, with his weak muscles, would have had great difficulty doing that, so this time; Dr. K. suggested that he give Tom the lethal injection.

"Lloyd and I never forgot that intense interview, so when he asked me to check with Henry to see if there were currently any drugs he could take to assist in his own suicide, I knew he was serious. This end-of-life matter I was well aware of and had researched and studied because of my work with the elderly.

"Some states were having a hard time getting a doctor-assisted suicide bill passed. Just last year, in 2009, politicians sparred over a provision in the Affordable Care Act concerning end-of-life consultations, called 'death panels' by critics, to help control health-care costs. I learned that about 28 percent, or *170 billion dollars,* of Medicare is spent just on patients' last six months of life, according to Medicare statistics.

"Only a very few states allow doctor-assisted suicide and this state is not one of them. Also, Lloyd didn't have a terminal illness so *no* doctor anywhere would help him—legally. I've heard that doctors do it but keep it quiet because of the laws. They don't want to be another Kevorkian--that strikes fear in them.

"So, I talked to Henry about drugs to help Lloyd. He listened quietly while I pled Lloyd's case telling him everything I knew about the laws and about Lloyd's situation, except about his fear of getting AIDS. Henry is so polite that I couldn't tell how he felt about what I was asking him to do. After that first talk, he said he'd need time to think about it. I told him to take all the time he needed.

"When he came to me a month later, he said he'd get me the drugs but he wanted three things from me: To never tell Maudine that he had helped me; for me not to help Lloyd take them—to just leave the pills on Lloyd's bedside table with a glass of water close by and leave the room; and he said to never tell him (Henry) what I had done with the pills—tossed them down the toilet or something else. I told him I could do this, so he got me the pills. I put them in a small plastic bag that couldn't be traced.

"What I *never* thought about is that Skip and Cindy, or Selena and Jack could be erroneously blamed for his death. There's just been so much talk about the possibility of them having something to do with his death. I never wanted this and I know Lloyd didn't either. So that's why I wanted you here, Tim. I need you to make a professional statement that Lloyd died of natural causes, or, at least, did not die a suspicious death. If I have to, I'll tell the world what I did to keep the young people from being harmed by this. So, will you help me?" Maude sat back in her chair, breathing heavily, with her eyes closed, and didn't say anything else.

Tim looked at her, stunned about her confession. He thought, *this little old woman is willing to tell the world what she did to keep the young family and even Selena safe. And I thought she didn't even like them, but, evidently, her values about fairness extend to them, too. She's quite a lady.*

Anna spoke first when she saw Tim needed time to think, "Aunt Maude, that had to be the hardest thing you've ever had to do. I don't know how you were able to do it."

Maude said, "Lloyd had become my best friend again once his two wives were gone. I guess he knew I would be there for him, no matter what. The fact that he could ask me to get him the drugs told me he trusted me. Also, I had never told anyone that he was *gay* and he appreciated that.

"We saw each other every day—he would bring me his Birmingham newspaper after he read it and we'd visit for a while. Once he went into the nursing home, I would get his newspaper every day and take it to him. The day I took him the pills was a very hard day for me. I put them on the bedside table with the newspaper covering them, told him they were there, set a glass of water nearby, hugged him and whispered that I'd see him soon, either here or in heaven, and then I walked out of the room and the building. I didn't cry until I got back home and in my bedroom. I didn't want Sukie to hear me and worry about me."

Tim now began to speak slowly, "Nothing will be gained by revealing what you've told us. We'll wait for the autopsy report and then tell the sheriff and townspeople that there were no signs of foul play. That's all we have to say since you had the autopsy done and will get the results. The later report will come directly to you, and if there's anything suspicious in it, you can destroy it. Sheriff Taylor is not going to insist on seeing the reports."

Anna breathed a sigh of relief. She got up from her chair and went over to Maude to hug her and comfort her. "That's over. Now, will you come to stay with us as soon as you can get everything arranged?"

Maude hugged her tight, then patted her and said, "We'll see."

CHAPTER 14

Two days later, Anna went out of the front door at Maude's house to get the mail from the mail box by the road. *It's 10 A.M. and is already a scorcher and probably almost as hot as hell is*, she thought as she took the mail out of the box. When she saw that the autopsy report was there, she ran back into the house and right to the kitchen where Maude was. "It's here, Aunt Maude, right on time." She handed all the mail to her with the autopsy report on top.

Anna followed Maude to the library where Tim was and Maude handed the report to him, in the unopened envelope. "You look at it first, Tim, and tell me what it says; I don't think I can read it anyway with my hands shaking so much."

Tim laid the book down that he was reading and took the unopened letter from her trembling fingers. He slit the envelope open and pulled the three-page report out. Anna thought, *it feels like this is taking place in slow motion, like in a movie where the frames were slowed down as though it will stop any second.* Then, she prayed silently, *Please, God, don't let the report show Tim anything that can get my Aunt Maude in trouble.*

After Tim read over the report slowly—too slowly in Anna's opinion—and then read it again, he looked over at the sofa where Maude and Anna were sitting and holding each other's hands.

He looked into Maude's eyes and said, "I don't see anything that can be construed as a suspicious death. After you read it and I answer any questions you may have, I'll take it to Sheriff Taylor's office and tell him what the autopsy shows. If he wants to see the report, I'll show it to him, but I'm thinking he's not even going to want to see it. I'm also thinking that if he knew what went down here, he wouldn't do anything to you, and would suggest that you not talk about it, nor worry about it any longer."

Maude shook her head, saying, "I don't even want to read it. Just take it away and do what you want with it. When the full report comes in, I'll keep it in my wall safe until you can see it, and then we're done with this. I just want to forget all about it; it's been a nightmare."

Tim turned to Anna, "Please get us on the next available flight to Chicago while I go talk to the sheriff. Maude, will you be okay if we leave now, and come back later to take you back with us? I know you won't go now until you're comfortable that Skip and his family are out of harm's way, but we want you with us as soon as you feel you can come stay with us." He got up and hugged her and Anna as he went out the door.

As Tim went out the door to the portico, Rich was coming up the drive-up. They greeted each other and Rich said, "I'm leaving now. Doesn't look like a way to stop the will as it is. I talked to Dad and he doesn't want me to pursue it. He thinks we're all getting some money and to try to get the will changed will only give the lawyers more and us less.

All he asks is that Skip and Cindy not spend it all and wants them to put some money in trust for their children's education. I've told Skip what Daddy Dan said and it's what Lloyd wanted, too. So I'm going in to say goodbye to Maude and tell her this, then I'm on my way out of this town for good." They said their goodbyes and Rich went on into the house.

Rich found Maude and Anna in the kitchen and told them what he had just told Tim. Rich and Anna exchanged e-mail addresses, he hugged them both, got his bag and left. *Well, that was a bummer*, he thought. *You just never know what family will do to each other, especially where money is concerned. Hope I get away from here without any further contacts.*

Tim called Sheriff Taylor on the way to his office and found him in. When he got there he told him the autopsy report was in and there were no signs of foul play. Tim held the envelope with the report out to the sheriff who declined to see it.

"I'll take your word for it; don't need to see the report. I never thought there was anything to all the gossip, but I'm glad you helped Miss Maude with it and glad you came down." Tim told him they were leaving but coming back later to take Maude back with them. He asked the sheriff to look in on her once in a while.

"You know I will. She probably told you I checked on her and Mr. Lloyd about once a month. If you want an update from me, just call." They exchanged cards and Tim was on his way.

As their plane took off from the Birmingham airport, Anna leaned back in her seat and breathed a big sigh of relief. "Well, that's over! I'm glad to leave that all behind us. I wish we were taking Aunt Maude with us this time, but it'll be easier when we come back to get her. And that time will not be in the heat of summer, I hope!

Tim said, "I hope it's soon. I want to get her away from there as soon as possible; certainly before someone gets wind of the autopsy reports."

"What do you mean? I thought you said it showed no suspicions," said Anna who reached for the envelope Tim was holding out to her, while she stared into his eyes. As she read the report, she looked at Tim who was looking straight ahead.

She whispered, "How did you do that? How did you get everyone to decline reading this report? It clearly says that several foreign substances were found in the body and names them. If the sheriff had read this he would have opened an investigation, wouldn't he?" She kept staring at Tim as he looked at her and smiled."

"I gambled and won—so far. So, we've got to get Maude away from Hamlin, soon. Hey, did you bring any of that Lane Cake with you? If you did, I want some as soon as we get home."

RECIPES from
SECRETS IN A SMALL SOUTHERN TOWN: A MYSTERY

Southern Comfort Food and Their Origins:
(Listed as they appear in the story)

Chicken-Fried Pork Chops
Brazilian Collards
Peach Cobbler
Lane Cake
Barbequed Pork
Alabama Brunswick Stew
Chicken and Dressing
Green Bean Casserole
Broccoli-Raisin Salad
Watermelon Rind Pickles
Homemade Rolls
Texas Sheet Cake
Kentucky Derby Pie
Southern Chocolate Pound Cake
Strawberry Cake
Southern Red Velvet Cake

T. = tablespoon
t. = teaspoon
These abbreviations will be used in all the
following recipes.

Chicken-Fried Pork Chops, Cream Gravy

I learned how to make this dish watching my mother and grandmother cook.

4 thin pork chops, or pound thick ones to ¼ inch thin. Season with salt and pepper. Mix together about 2 cups flour and a little salt and pepper in one bowl. Mix together 1 egg, and about ¾ cup milk in another bowl. Dip each chop in milk/egg mix, then in flour mix. Let sit 15-20 minutes, and then fry in hot oil about two minutes each side. When brown, drain on paper towels and keep warm.

MAKE GRAVY: In fry pan that chops were cooked in, drain off all but about 2 tablespoons oil, leaving brown bits in bottom. Add about 3 tablespoons flour from first bowl to fry pan and stir, making a roux. Pour in about 2½ cups hot milk (heat in Microwave). Reduce heat and simmer 'til thick (about 5 minutes). Season gravy, if needed, and put over pork chops and mashed potatoes, or hot biscuits.

Brazilian Collards

I got this recipe, a typed version which I still have, from Bill Earle, Executive Director of the Children's Home Society of Florida back in 1985, when I began working with him on adoptions in Orlando. He was a great cook and a great director.

This recipe replaced my family's Alabama version of adding a square piece of "streak-o'-lean" meat in the pot with the collards and salt. Cover with water and cook for a few hours.

"Mess" of collard greens

2–3 T. olive oil
2 – 3 medium onions
4 – 5 cloves garlic
Pinch of sugar
salt to taste
1 can (15 – 16 oz.) chicken broth

Strip, wash, and slightly chop collards. Drain and blot with a towel to remove as much moisture as possible.

Dice onions and sauté in olive oil in wok, electric fry pan or Dutch oven on medium heat.

Add finely chopped garlic and stir in with onions.

Add well-drained collards and stir fry for 5 to 10 minutes until totally wilted.

Add chicken broth, sugar, and very little salt. Simmer for ½ to ¾ hour, stirring occasionally, until liquid is almost gone.

Let the greens "cure" for 4 – 5 hours or overnight. They get better with age.

My Quick Version of Brazilian Collards:

16 oz. package frozen chopped collards- cook 20 minutes in pressure cooker or microwave oven, then drain.

Saute: large onion, chopped
3 cloves garlic, chopped
2 T. oil.
Add: drained collards,
pinch of sugar and salt;
15-16 oz. can chicken broth.

Cook until liquid almost gone. Add dashes of vinegar to taste.

Deep-Dish Georgia Peach Cobbler ~ *My recipe from the early '60s. This can be made with canned peaches but the fresh ripe Georgia peaches are especially delicious.*

Preheat oven to 350 degrees.

5 - 6 cups fresh ripe Georgia peaches

1 t. almond extract

2 cups sugar

2 T. lemon juice

Peel and slice peaches into a 2-quart or larger oven-proof dish. Combine other ingredients immediately and mix with peaches to keep peaches from turning brown.

Mix and pour over peaches:

1 ½ cups plain flour

½ t. salt

3 t. baking powder

2 T. sugar

1 egg, beaten lightly

1 cup milk

Dot with 2-3 tablespoons butter on top. Sprinkle with cinnamon/sugar mix.

Bake 45 minutes at 350 degrees.

Serve warm with vanilla ice cream on top.

LANE CAKE-- *History and Recipe for a Classic Boozy Layer Cake: "Miss Maudie Atkinson baked a Lane cake so loaded with *shinny it made me tight." from the book, To Kill a Mockingbird. by Harper Lee(1960), a native of Monroeville, Alabama.*

*shinny = slang for moonshine

Emma Rylander Lane (d. April 25, 1904) of Clayton, Alabama, introduced the now classic treat bearing her name in her self-published and extremely hard to find 1898 cookbook, A Few Good Things to Eat (the easier-to-find 1989 reprint was renamed Some Good Things to Eat). In her book, Mrs. Lane titled the concoction "Prize Cake," as it had won first prize at a baking contest at a country fair in Columbus, Georgia – about 60 miles from her home in Americus. The concoction eventually took on the name of its creator.

Lane Cake is a three-or-four-layer white cake with a thick bourbon-laced raisin filling. The egg whites are used for making the vanilla butter cake and the egg yolks for the custard filling.

The recipe is on next three pages.

Lane Cake-Batter Ingredients:

3 ½ sifted cake flour

or 3 cups all-purpose flour

3 ½ t. baking powder

1/8 t. salt

¼ t. grated nutmeg (optional)

2 cups granulated sugar

1 cup unsalted soft butter(2 sticks)

1 t. vanilla extract

½ t. almond extract

1 cup milk

8 large egg whites

Combine dry ingredients. Combine wet ingredients. Using an electric mixer, combine the two together starting and ending with dry ingredients. Beat several minutes. Bake in 2-3 prepared pans 350 degrees for 20 minutes then test for doneness.

Lane Cake-Filling Between Layers:

8 large egg yolks

1 ¼ cups granulated sugar

½ cup unsalted soft butter (1 stick)

¼ t. salt

½ cup bourbon or brandy

1 t. vanilla extract

1 cup finely chopped raisins

1 cup finely chopped pecans

1 cup grated fresh coconut,(optional)

½ cup finely chopped candied maraschino
cherries or pineapple (optional)

Mix and beat together egg yolks, sugar, butter, salt, bourbon or brandy, and vanilla. Fold in raisins, pecans, coconut, and other fruit. Mix together and put between cooled cake layers.

Lane Cake-Boiled Frosting:

1 cup granulated sugar

1/3 cup water

2 large egg whites

Pinch salt, or ¼ t. cream of tartar

1 t. vanilla extract

In a saucepan, stir together the sugar, water and salt or cream of tartar. Cook over medium-high heat until the sugar is dissolved and the mixture is bubbly.

In a medium mixing bowl, whip the egg whites and vanilla to soft peaks. Gradually add the sugar mixture while whipping constantly until stiff peaks form, about 7 to 10 minutes. Frost the cake.

You will also need:

three 9- by 1½-inch round baking pans or two 9- by 3-inch round baking pans or spring-form pans, parchment paper, mixing bowls, stand mixer or hand mixer, cooling rack, 2-quart saucepan, wooden spoon, candy thermometer.

Servings: One 9-inch, 4 or 3-layer cake, 12 to 16 servings

Alabama Brunswick Stew ~ *I got this recipe in the '50s from my mother-in-law, Pauline, who had been a home-economics (home-ec.) teacher at Valley High School in Alabama years before. Many of my recipes are from her. She was a super cook; she would make this stew in big batches and freeze it in quart containers for use later. Don, my husband, and I attended a funeral a few years back in our hometown and found this same recipe still being served.*

I remember, as a young child, attending a family reunion where Brunswick stew was made in the big black, laundry wash-pot outside over a fire.

2 chickens
6.5 lbs. pork roast
4 lbs. beef roast
15 onions, peeled
3-15 oz. cans cream corn
3-15 oz. cans tomatoes
3 small bottles ketchup
15 cups broth from the meats

Cook meats, cool.
Grind meats and onions.
   (or use frozen chopped onions).

Add tomatoes, ketchup, broth and simmer several
hours, stirring often.

Add corn and cook until thick.

Makes about 10 quarts.

Chicken and Cornbread Dressing ~ *I have been making dressing for my family for so many years that I don't remember where the original recipe came from, possibly from an Auburn University Cookbook. I've adapted it many times over the years and currently use this one.*

Stew a 4-pound or larger hen or fryer until done and falling off the bones. Use this broth to make dressing and gravy. You can also bake a turkey or hen, then you will need more chicken broth for the dressing, so have about 2-3 quarts on standby if you bake the bird.

For Dressing:

Make cornbread with 1 cup self-rising meal, 1 egg, 2 T. vegetable or peanut oil, milk to moisten. Bake about 20 minutes 350 degrees, or until done. When cool, crumble into very large bowl.

Add large bag Pepperidge Farm Herb Stuffing Mix, 1 cup dry powdered milk, 2-4 T. poultry seasoning (or more to taste), salt, pepper, and MSG (optional).

While cornbread cooks, dice 2 large onions, 2 large stalks celery, add 1 cup chicken broth.

Microwave 2 minutes. Cool slightly then add to dry ingredients with 4 lightly beaten eggs, and enough chicken broth to make "soupy mix" of the cornbread mix in large bowl. Bake in 2-3 prepared pans at 400 degrees for 35-40 minutes. You can bake some of the dressing in muffin tins for a shorter time.

Chicken or Turkey Gravy ~ Make roux with 1 stick butter, 3 T. flour. Stir together in 2-quart saucepan over medium heat until starts to turn brown. Add 1 quart chicken broth, or more, and salt and pepper to taste.

Slice or shred chicken and serve with dressing and gravy.

(My daughter, Jane has continued to adapt this recipe, and adds a can of cream of chicken soup to the dressing mix. She also has cooked it in a large crock pot to save room in the oven for other things. She cooks her cornbread the night before to save time.)

Pauline's Green Bean Casserole ~ This is *another of my mother-in-law's recipes. I got this from her in 1979 and we all like it. Some cooks leave out the sprouts and add more green beans.*

Sauté ¼ stick butter & 1 chopped onion and
Add: 1 can cream of mushroom soup
1 small jar cut pimentos
1 can chopped water chestnuts
1 package chopped or slivered almonds, browned
Mix together.

In large casserole dish, sprayed with *Pam*, put:
1 quart canned green beans, drained
1 can bean sprouts, drained
Or 2 quarts green beans

Pour soup mix over beans and mix well. Bake 30 minutes at 350 degrees. (or Microwave 10 minutes).
Top with ½ cup grated cheese and
1 can French-Fried Onion Rings
Bake another 10 - 15 minutes (or Microwave 5 minutes)

Sue Ellen's Broccoli-Raisin Salad ~ *I got this recipe from a co-worker in Tuscaloosa. I think it's the original and the way I fix it. Some cooks now add things like cheese, or Bacos rather than fresh bacon.*

1 bunch broccoli-use only the florets
½ cup red onion, sliced thin and separated into rings
1 cup golden raisins
1 cup mayonnaise
½ cup sugar

I "pre-plump" the raisins by mixing with mayo and sugar.

Cook the bacon. I microwave it until crisp. Toss together florets and onion and add mayo/raisin mix just before serving. Top with bacon.

WATERMELON RIND PICKLES ~ *I adapted this from a recipe I found in "Winning Seasons" a cookbook created by the Junior League in Tuscaloosa, Alabama, 1979. They have given me permission to use the recipe in this book.*

The title, "Winning Seasons", refers to the University of Alabama's winning football team, coached by "Bear" Bryant, at that time. The last time I made these pickles was in July, 1991, when we had lots of watermelons. Later, at Christmas, I gave jars of the pickles as gifts to co-workers.

(I doubled this recipe to have plenty for gift-giving.)

2 lbs. prepared watermelon rinds
Lime water made from 1 quart water
1 T. builder's lime
1 quart clear, distilled vinegar, divided
1 cup water
5 cups sugar (2.5 lbs.)
1 T. whole allspice
1 T. whole cloves
6 small pieces stick cinnamon

1. Trim green skin and pink portions from watermelon. Cut in small pieces (about 1"x 1"), or larger if desired. Soak 2-3 hours in lime water. Drain & rinse rind. Cover in cold water & boil 1 hour, or until tender.
2. Drain the watermelon and cover with weak vinegar solution (1 cup vinegar, 2 cups water), and let stand overnight.
3. Next day, discard liquid. Make syrup of 3 cups vinegar, 1 cup water, sugar, and spices. Heat to simmering point, remove from heat, cover, and steep for 1 hour to extract flavor from spices.
4. Add the drained watermelon to syrup and cook gently for 2 hours, or until syrup is fairly thick.
5. Pack in sterilized pint standard canning jars. Adjust lids and process in boiling water bath canner (212 degrees F.) for 15 minutes.

Note: Must be cooked in enamel or stainless steel or pickles will turn dark.

Recipe contributed by Mrs. Haskell Nevin

If you want lots of southern recipes, I recommend this book: "Winning Seasons." You can order it. Google: Junior League of Tuscaloosa for their website.

Pauline's Yeast Rolls ~ *We would make a big batch of these and keep the dough in the refrigerator, taking out small amounts to make up the rolls, shaping in various ways, let them rise, and then bake at 350 degrees until brown.*

4 cups milk, scalded	10 cups plain flour
1 cup sugar	1 T. salt
1 cup shortening	1 t. soda
1 package yeast	1 t. baking powder

Dissolve yeast in ¼ cup lukewarm water. Mix together milk, sugar, shortening, and add yeast.

Add 6 cups flour, mix and let rise until doubled.

Add salt, soda, baking powder to 4 cups flour. You can make into rolls now, or refrigerator until needed.

Eleanor's Rolls ~ *A friend in Orlando, originally from Robertsdale, Alabama, made her rolls differently and they were also good.*

3 eggs and ½ cup melted butter ~ put in pint jar and add scalded milk (cooled then fill jar).

Dissolve 1 package yeast in ½ cup warm water and a teaspoon sugar.

Put liquids in large bowl, add 1 t. salt, 1 cup sugar.

Add flour (no amount given) and gradually blend in flour until dough doesn't stick to hands. Knead 10 minutes. Cover and let rise until doubled.

Knead 1 minute, shape into rolls, let rise, then bake at 350 degrees until brown.

Aline's Texas Sheet Cake ~ *I got this recipe from a good friend in Tuscaloosa, another great cook. It's so easy to make.*

2 cups sugar
2 cups flour ~ sift together in large bowl.

2 sticks butter
4 T. cocoa
1 cup water ~ bring to boil, pour over sugar and flour.

Add: ½ cup buttermilk (make buttermilk by mixing 2 T. lemon juice & regular milk to ½ cup measure).

Add: 2 eggs, lightly beaten
1 t. baking soda
1 t. cinnamon
1 t. vanilla flavoring.
Pour in greased 11x14 pan and bake 20 minutes at 400 degrees.

Icing for Sheet Cake ~ Mix, bring to boil: stick butter, 1
4 T. cocoa
6 T. milk.
Take off stove and add 1 pound box confectioners' sugar and 1 t. vanilla.
Beat until smooth. Add 1 cup chopped pecans.
Spread on cake while warm.

Pauline's Kentucky Derby Pie ~ This is

another easy recipe and so good. The recipe said you can add ½ cup bourbon, but my Southern Baptist mother-in-law never did (I don't think).

1. Put ¾ cup chocolate chips & ¾ cup pecans each into 2 unbaked pie shells.

2. Combine 4 eggs & 2 cups sugar. Beat until light.

3. Add in order given: 2 sticks melted butter
   2 t. vanilla extract
   1 cup plain flour

4. Pour over chips & nuts.

5. Bake 325 degrees for 40-45 minutes.

6. Top with whipped cream to serve.

Southern Chocolate Pound Cake ~ *Another recipe from a coworker, Kathy, in Tuscaloosa. We ate well at work.*

1½ cups butter (3 sticks)

3 cups sugar

4-5 large eggs

3 cups plain or cake flour

½ t. baking powder

¼ t. salt

5-6 heaping T. cocoa

1 cup milk

2 t. vanilla extract

¾ t. butter flavoring

Cream butter and sugar.

Add eggs, one at a time, beating one minute after each.

Add dry ingredients, & milk alternately.

Stir in vanilla & butter flavoring.

Bake in greased tube pan, Bundt pan or 2 loaf pans.

300-325 degrees, 1¼ - 1½ hours--Less time for loaf pans. Cool and loosen from sides before removing from pan.

Aunt Ollie's Strawberry Cake ~ *We first had this cake at a wedding party in Pensacola in 1965. It became popular fast because of the ease of making, nice color, and its yummy taste.*

1 white cake mix
½ package thawed/drained strawberries
½ cup water
½ cup vegetable oil
4 eggs
1 small package strawberry Jell-O

Blend all the above for 4 minutes in mixer bowl. Put in greased tube pan or 2-3 layer pans.

Bake 325 degrees 1 hour, 5 minutes (tube pan), or 20 minutes for layers. Pour juice from strawberries over cake.

Icing: 1 box confectioners' sugar
1 stick butter
½ package thawed/drained strawberries
red food color

Mix all together and beat until fluffy. Ice the cake. Only use enough food color for pink shade.

Southern Red Velvet Cake ~ *My daughter, Jane got this recipe from a former co-worker in Columbus, Georgia in 1978. Jane loves to cook and has many good southern recipes.*

1 ½ cups sugar

½ cup shortening, or 1 cup butter, softened

2 eggs

2 T. cocoa powder

2 (1 oz) bottles red food coloring

2 ½ cups plain flour

¾ t. salt

1 cup buttermilk, or substitute 1 T. vinegar mixed with enough milk to equal 1 cup

1 t. vanilla

1 t. baking soda

1 t. vinegar

Preheat oven to 350 degrees.

Prepare 3 round cake pans, greasing with shortening and dusting with flour or sifted cocoa powder.

Cream sugar and shortening (or butter) in mixer until light and fluffy. Add eggs, one at a time, and beat 1 minute after adding each one. Make a paste of cocoa powder and food color and add to sugar mixture. Mix flour and salt and add to mixing bowl, alternating with buttermilk, one half to one third at a time.

Add vanilla.

Mix baking soda and vinegar in separate cups and <u>stir</u> into cake mixture.(Do not use mixer.) Divide mixture evenly into 3 prepared cake pans.

Bake 350 degrees for 20-25 minutes.

Remove from oven when inserted toothpick comes out clean and let cool on rack while preparing frosting.

Red Velvet Cake Frosting

Ermine Icing – a French-style butter roux icing, aka Boiled Milk Frosting (Cream Cheese Icing is good but this recipe is worth the extra effort and time to make it!!!)

7 ½ T. flour

1 ½ cups milk

1 ½ t. vanilla extract

1 ½ cups butter

1 ½ cups sugar

Remove from heat, whisk in vanilla, and set aside to cool.

Beat butter and sugar together using mixer until fluffy.

Add cooled flour/milk mixture to butter/sugar mixture a little at a time and beat on medium until light and fluffy.

Slice each of the 3 cooled cake layers horizontally into 2 pieces-use dental floss.
Frost cake between the 6 layers and the top and sides.

***Even though I don't have any recipes of my mother's or grandmothers' (except the chicken fried pork chops) in the book, they were good cooks. I don't think my mother nor my two grandmothers ever had a measuring cup or measuring spoon, but everything they cooked turned out great. Yum. Good memories of Southern comfort foods.

Printed in the United States
By Bookmasters